Periodic GCSE Science revision from CGP!

There's a lot to learn for AQA's Grade 9-1 GCSE Combined Science exams... sometimes it can be hard to get motivated for a big revision session.

That's why we've made this fantastic book — it's brimming with bite-sized tests covering every topic from the Foundation Level course. And since they only take ten minutes each, they won't take over your life (unless you're really keen).

To round things off, all the answers are included at the back, along with a chart to keep track of your marks. It's a brilliant revision companion!

CGP — still the best ☺

Our sole aim here at CGP is to produce the highest quality books
— carefully written, immaculately presented and
dangerously close to being funny.

Then we work our socks off to get them out to you
— at the cheapest possible prices.

Published by CGP

Editors:
Sarah Armstrong, Charlotte Burrows, Daniel Fielding, Emily Garrett, Sharon Keeley-Holden, Charles Kitts, Duncan Lindsay, and Ethan Starmer-Jones.

ISBN: 978 1 78294 848 3

With thanks to Susan Alexander, Barrie Crowther, Emily Forsberg, Ian Francis, Glenn Rogers and Sarah Williams for the proofreading.
With thanks to Emily Smith for the copyright research.

Clipart from Corel®
Illustrations by: Sandy Gardner Artist, email sandy@sandygardner.co.uk
Printed by Bell & Bain Ltd, Glasgow.

Based on the classic CGP style created by Richard Parsons.

Text, design, layout and original illustrations © Coordination Group Publications Ltd. (CGP) 2017
All rights reserved.

Photocopying this book is not permitted, even if you have a CLA licence.
Extra copies are available from CGP with next day delivery • 0800 1712 712 • www.cgpbooks.co.uk

Contents

Biology Paper 1
Test 1: Cell Biology 2
Test 2: Organisation 4
Test 3: Organisation 6
Test 4: Infection and Response 8
Test 5: Infection and Response 10
Test 6: Bioenergetics 12
Test 7: Bioenergetics 14
Test 8: Biology 1 Mixed Topics 16
Test 9: Biology 1 Mixed Topics 18

Biology Paper 2
Test 10: Homeostasis and Response 20
Test 11: Homeostasis and Response 22
Test 12: Inheritance, Variation and Evolution 24
Test 13: Inheritance, Variation and Evolution 26
Test 14: Ecology 28
Test 15: Ecology 30
Test 16: Biology 2 Mixed Topics 32
Test 17: Biology 2 Mixed Topics 34

Chemistry Paper 1
Test 18: Atomic Structure and the Periodic Table 36
Test 19: Bonding, Structure and Properties 38
Test 20: Bonding, Structure and Properties 40
Test 21: Quantitative Chemistry 42
Test 22: Chemical Changes 44
Test 23: Energy Changes 46
Test 24: Chemistry 1 Mixed Topics 48
Test 25: Chemistry 1 Mixed Topics 50

Chemistry Paper 2
Test 26: Rate and Extent of Chemical Change 52
Test 27: Rate and Extent of Chemical Change 54
Test 28: Organic Chemistry 56
Test 29: Chemical Analysis 58
Test 30: Chemistry of the Atmosphere 60
Test 31: Chemistry of the Atmosphere 62
Test 32: Using Resources 64
Test 33: Chemistry 2 Mixed Topics 66
Test 34: Chemistry 2 Mixed Topics 68

Physics Paper 1
Test 35: Energy 70
Test 36: Energy 72
Test 37: Electricity 74
Test 38: Electricity 76
Test 39: Particle Model of Matter 78
Test 40: Atomic Structure 80
Test 41: Physics 1 Mixed Topics 82
Test 42: Physics 1 Mixed Topics 84

Physics Paper 2
Test 43: Forces 86
Test 44: Forces 88
Test 45: Forces 90
Test 46: Waves 92
Test 47: Waves 94
Test 48: Magnetism and Electromagnetism 96
Test 49: Physics 2 Mixed Topics 98
Test 50: Physics 2 Mixed Topics 100

Answers 102

Progress Chart 111

Test 1: Cell Biology

There are **12 questions** in this test. Give yourself **10 minutes** to answer them all.

1. When air is breathed in...
   - A ... oxygen is taken into the bloodstream and carbon dioxide is passed out.
   - B ... carbon dioxide is taken into the bloodstream and oxygen is passed out.

   [1]

2. True or False? "In human body cells, chromosomes usually come in pairs."
   - A True
   - B False

   [1]

3. Which process involves the movement of water only?
   - A Diffusion
   - B Osmosis
   - C Active transport

   [1]

4. When using a light microscope to view a slide, which lens should be selected to start with?
   - A Lowest-powered objective lens
   - B Highest-powered objective lens

   [1]

5. Chloroplasts...
   - A ... strengthen a plant cell.
   - B ... store the genetic material of a cell.
   - C ... absorb light energy to make glucose.

   [1]

6. Which of these characteristics makes the alveoli efficient at gas exchange?
   - A They have thick walls.
   - B They have a large surface area.

   [1]

7. Which of these parts are not found in a bacterial cell?
   - A Nucleus
   - B Cell membrane
   - C Cell wall

   [1]

8. True or False? "Mitosis results in two cells that are genetically different."
   - A True
   - B False

   [1]

9. Give one condition that embryonic stem cells could be used to treat.

....
[1]

10. A nerve cell carries electrical impulses.
Give one way that a nerve cell is adapted for its job.

....
[1]

11. Why can't a root hair cell absorb mineral ions from the soil by diffusion?

....

....

What process do root hair cells use to absorb mineral ions from the soil?

....
[2]

12. Complete this diagram of an animal cell.

What role do mitochondria have in the cell?

....

....
[3]

Test 2: Organisation

There are **13 questions** in this test. Give yourself **10 minutes** to answer them all.

1. What is a tissue?

   A A collection of different types of cell that work together.

   B A collection of similar cells that work together.

   [1]

2. What colour is iodine solution in the presence of starch?

   A Blue-black

   B Browny-orange

   [1]

3. True or False? "Blood is a tissue."

   A True

   B False

   [1]

4. What artificial device can be used to keep arteries open and blood flowing?

   A A ventilator

   B A valve

   C A stent

   [1]

5. Which type of tumour is cancerous?

   A Benign

   B Malignant

   [1]

6. Which of these is a chamber of the heart?

   A Aorta

   B Right atrium

   C Vena cava

   [1]

7. Bile is produced in the...

   A ... liver.

   B ... gall bladder.

   C ... stomach.

   [1]

8. What's the function of palisade mesophyll tissue?

   A It's where photosynthesis happens.

   B It carries substances around a plant.

   [1]

Biology Paper 1: Organisation

9. Give one risk factor that can increase a person's chance of developing liver disease.

   ....
   [1]

10. How does increased air movement around a plant's leaves affect the rate of transpiration?

    ....
    [1]

11. What is the role of protease enzymes?

    ....

    ....
    [1]

12. What happens to an enzyme if the temperature is too high?

    ....

    How does this affect how well the enzyme works?

    ....
    [2]

13. Give two components of blood that are carried in the blood plasma.

    1. ....

    2. ....
    [2]

Test 3: Organisation

There are **12 questions** in this test. Give yourself **10 minutes** to answer them all.

1. True or False? "Organ systems work together to form organs."

   A True

   B False

   [1]

2. True or False? "Xylem tissue transports dissolved sugars around a plant."

   A True

   B False

   [1]

3. Which of the following would you use to test for the presence of protein?

   A Biuret solution

   B Benedict's solution

   [1]

4. What is the function of white blood cells?

   A They transport deoxygenated blood around the body.

   B They defend the body against microorganisms.

   [1]

5. Why is the shape of an enzyme important for its function?

   A So that it can enter the cells of the body.

   B So that it fits the substance involved in the reaction it is catalysing.

   [1]

6. What is the name of the cells that control the opening and closing of stomata?

   A Palisade cells

   B Guard cells

   C Meristem cells

   [1]

7. People who have problems with their immune system have...

   A ... an increased chance of suffering from communicable diseases.

   B ... a decreased chance of suffering from communicable diseases.

   [1]

8. Which word describes the loss of water from a plant's surface?

   A Transpiration

   B Translocation

   [1]

Biology Paper 1: Organisation © CGP — not to be photocopied

9. The heart contains cells that act as a pacemaker.
Where are these cells located in the heart?

   ....
   [1]

10. Disease can negatively affect a person's physical and mental health.
Give two other factors that can do this.

   1. ....

   2. ....
   [2]

11. Give two differences between arteries and veins.

   1. ....

   ....

   2. ....

   ....
   [2]

12. What effect do statins have on cholesterol in the blood?

   ....

   What disease do statins help reduce the risk of a person getting?

   ....
   [2]

Test 4: Infection and Response

There are **13 questions** in this test. Give yourself **10 minutes** to answer them all.

1. What is the first stage of testing a new medicinal drug?
   A   The drug is tested on human cells and tissues in the lab.
   B   The drug is tested on human volunteers in a clinical trial.
   [1]

2. How does the stomach help to defend the body against pathogens?
   A   It secretes hydrochloric acid to kill pathogens.
   B   It secretes antibodies to kill pathogens.
   [1]

3. What's a microorganism that causes disease called?
   A   An antibody
   B   An antitoxin
   C   A pathogen
   [1]

4. True or False? "For a large outbreak of an infectious disease to be prevented, everyone must be vaccinated against it."
   A   True
   B   False
   [1]

5. Which drug was discovered by Alexander Fleming?
   A   Penicillin
   B   Aspirin
   [1]

6. Gonorrhoea is a disease caused by...
   A   ... protists.
   B   ... viruses.
   C   ... bacteria.
   [1]

7. True or False? "Antibiotics can kill viruses."
   A   True
   B   False
   [1]

8. Which type of drugs are used to control HIV?
   A   Antibiotics
   B   Antiretrovirals
   [1]

Biology Paper 1: Infection and Response

9. Which plant does digitalis originally come from?

   ....
   [1]

10. Give one way in which rose black spot disease can be treated.

    ....
    [1]

11. Tobacco mosaic virus causes a mosaic pattern of discolouration on a plant's leaves. Explain why this affects plant growth.

    ....

    ....
    [1]

12. How does the nose help to defend the body against disease?

    ....

    ....
    [2]

13. Give two ways to help to prevent the spread of malaria.

    1. ....

    2. ....
    [2]

Test 5: Infection and Response

There are **12 questions** in this test. Give yourself **10 minutes** to answer them all.

1. What is a placebo?

   A A name given to the drug being tested in a clinical trial.

   B A substance that looks like the drug being tested, but that doesn't do anything.

   [1]

2. Which of these statements about bacteria is true?

   A Bacteria damage cells by living and replicating inside them.

   B Some bacteria reproduce really quickly in the body.

   [1]

3. True or False? "Painkillers can be used to kill pathogens."

   A True

   B False

   [1]

4. Which disease are young children often vaccinated against?

   A HIV

   B Salmonella food poisoning

   C Measles

   [1]

5. Phagocytosis is the process in which white blood cells...

   A ...engulf and digest foreign cells.

   B ...release antitoxins.

   [1]

6. Which of the following diseases is caused by a protist?

   A Measles

   B Malaria

   C HIV

   [1]

7. True or False? "Preclinical trials help to find the optimum dose for a drug."

   A True

   B False

   [1]

8. Which type of pathogen causes rose black spot?

   A A fungus

   B A bacterium

   C A virus

   [1]

Biology Paper 1: Infection and Response

9. What is an antibiotic?

    ....
    [1]

10. How is the measles virus spread between people?

    ....

    ....
    [1]

11. Where do viruses live and replicate in the body?

    ....

    How do viruses make a person feel ill?

    ....

    ....
    [2]

12. Explain how vaccination can protect against a disease.

    ....

    ....

    ....

    ....
    [3]

Test 6: Bioenergetics

There are **12 questions** in this test. Give yourself **10 minutes** to answer them all.

1. During exercise, which of the following happens?
   A   Just your breathing rate increases.
   B   Just your breath volume increases.
   C   Your breathing rate and your breath volume increase.
   [1]

2. Which of the following could you use to measure the rate of photosynthesis in pondweed?
   A   The rate of oxygen production.
   B   The rate of water uptake.
   [1]

3. True or False? "Aerobic respiration occurs in plants and animals all the time."
   A   True
   B   False
   [1]

4. Which of these factors affects the rate of photosynthesis?
   A   Amount of soil
   B   Nitrogen concentration
   C   Light intensity
   [1]

5. Which type of respiration transfers more energy?
   A   Aerobic respiration
   B   Anaerobic respiration
   [1]

6. Respiration is an...
   A   ...exothermic reaction.
   B   ...endothermic reaction.
   [1]

7. What process occurs in yeast to make bread?
   A   Fermentation
   B   Transpiration
   C   Photosynthesis
   [1]

8. True or False? "The starch in plants that's created from glucose is insoluble."
   A   True
   B   False
   [1]

Biology Paper 1: Bioenergetics

9. Why do muscles start respiring anaerobically during vigorous exercise?

   ....

   ....
   [1]

10. Name the supporting material that plants make using glucose.

    ....

    Which part of the cell is made using this material?

    ....
    [2]

11. Complete the equation for photosynthesis.

    ....

    .... + water ⟶ .... + oxygen
    [2]

12. Respiration releases energy. Give two uses of this energy.

    1. ....

    ....

    2. ....

    ....
    [2]

Test 7: Bioenergetics

There are **12 questions** in this test. Give yourself **10 minutes** to answer them all.

1. True or False? "Anaerobic respiration requires oxygen."
   A True
   B False
   [1]

2. Alex walked to catch the bus, but Peter was late so had to run. Who would have had the higher heart rate?
   A Alex
   B Peter
   [1]

3. Which of these things is used by plants to make proteins?
   A Nitrate ions
   B Lipids
   C Cellulose
   [1]

4. Other than oxygen, what does photosynthesis produce?
   A Carbon dioxide
   B Glucose
   C Water
   [1]

5. True or False? "As the level of carbon dioxide increases, the rate of photosynthesis will always increase."
   A True
   B False
   [1]

6. Which chemical symbol represents glucose?
   A $C_6H_{12}O_6$
   B CO_2
   [1]

7. Which of the following is produced when yeast cells respire anaerobically?
   A Glucose
   B Ethanol
   [1]

8. True or False? "A single lipid molecule is made from one glycerol molecule and three fatty acid molecules."
   A True
   B False
   [1]

Biology Paper 1: Bioenergetics

© CGP — not to be photocopied

9. What is meant by the term 'metabolism'?

   ....

   ....
   [1]

10. What happens to the rate of photosynthesis if a plant is put in a dark place?

    ....

    Explain your answer.

    ....

    ....
    [2]

11. What is muscle fatigue?

    ....

    ....

    When does muscle fatigue occur?

    ....
    [2]

12. Lots of glucose molecules can be joined together to form bigger molecules in a cell. Name two of these bigger molecules that can be made in a plant cell.

    1. ....

    2. ....
    [2]

Test 8: Biology 1 Mixed Topics

There are **12 questions** in this test. Give yourself **10 minutes** to answer them all.

1. Phloem is made up of...

    A ... hollow tubes of dead cells strengthened by lignin.

    B ... columns of elongated cells with small pores in the end walls.

    [1]

2. Why is a new drug tested on live animals?

    A To test how well the drug works compared to a placebo.

    B To test for safety before testing the drug on humans.

    [1]

3. What is the function of the cell wall?

    A To strengthen the cell.

    B To make proteins.

    C To help with respiration.

    [1]

4. True or False? "Active transport means that cells can absorb minerals against a concentration gradient."

    A True

    B False

    [1]

5. Chromosomes are...

    A ... a type of organelle where photosynthesis occurs.

    B ... really long molecules of DNA, which contain genes.

    [1]

6. The leaf is an example of a plant...

    A ... tissue.

    B ... organ.

    C ... organ system.

    [1]

7. The 'lock and key' model is used to describe...

    A ... the rate of diffusion.

    B ... the action of enzymes.

    [1]

8. True or False? "The DNA in plant cells is found within a nucleus."

    A True

    B False

    [1]

9. Complete this equation for magnification.

$$\text{magnification} = \frac{\text{..}}{\text{..}}$$

[1]

10. Give two ways that an exchange surface in animals may be specialised for its function.

1. ....

2. ....

[2]

11. A student investigates the effect of pH on the reaction rate of amylase on starch solution. Give one example of a variable that must be controlled in this investigation.

....

How could this variable be controlled?

....

[2]

12. Explain how having a large surface area affects the rate of diffusion across an exchange surface.

....

....

....

[2]

15

Test 9: Biology 1 Mixed Topics

There are **12 questions** in this test. Give yourself **10 minutes** to answer them all.

1. Which part of the blood is used to clot blood at wounds?
   - A Red blood cells
   - B White blood cells
   - C Platelets

   [1]

2. Which of the following plant tissues can differentiate into lots of different types of cell?
   - A Epidermal tissue
   - B Meristem tissue

   [1]

3. What happens at the end of mitosis?
   - A The cytoplasm and cell membrane divide to form two identical cells.
   - B DNA is replicated to form two copies of each chromosome.

   [1]

4. How are root cells specialised for absorbing water and nutrients?
   - A They are round.
   - B The cells are shaped like long hairs.

   [1]

5. True or False? "Some types of cancer can be triggered by a viral infection."
   - A True
   - B False

   [1]

6. What is a cell called when it has differentiated?
   - A A specialised cell.
   - B A stem cell.

   [1]

7. Some of the glucose from photosynthesis is used for...
   - A ... transpiration.
   - B ... respiration.

   [1]

8. If you place a slice of potato in a solution that has a higher sugar concentration, the potato will...
   - A ... release water and decrease in mass.
   - B ... absorb water and increase in mass.

   [1]

Biology Paper 1: Mixed Topics

9. Name one non-specific defence system of the human body.

....
[1]

10. Name the blood vessel that carries blood from the lungs to the heart.

....

Name the blood vessel that carries blood from the heart to the organs.

....
[2]

11. Give two examples of diseases that can be caused directly by smoking.

1. ....

2. ....
[2]

12. In coronary heart disease, layers of fatty material build up inside the coronary arteries, narrowing them. Explain how this affects the heart muscle.

....

....

....
[2]

Biology Paper 2

Test 10: Homeostasis and Response

There are **12 questions** in this test. Give yourself **10 minutes** to answer them all.

1. Reflex actions are...

   A ... automatic actions.

   B ... conscious actions.

   [1]

2. True or False? "The contraceptive implant continuously releases oestrogen."

   A True

   B False

   [1]

3. What is secreted by the pancreas when blood glucose levels rise?

   A Insulin

   B Glycogen

   [1]

4. Where in the body would you find the adrenal glands?

   A In the neck

   B In the brain

   C Just above the kidneys

   [1]

5. Secondary sex characteristics develop...

   A ... during the menstrual cycle.

   B ... at puberty.

   [1]

6. True or False? "The pituitary gland secretes hormones that regulate body conditions."

   A True

   B False

   [1]

7. What is the central nervous system made up of?

   A The brain and receptors

   B The brain and the spinal cord

   C The spinal cord and receptors

   [1]

8. The process where an egg is released from the ovary is called...

   A ... maturation.

   B ... ovulation.

   [1]

Biology Paper 2: Homeostasis and Response

9. What is the role of a receptor in the nervous system?

....
[1]

10. Type 1 diabetes is where the pancreas doesn't produce enough insulin. It may not produce any insulin at all. Why is Type 1 diabetes dangerous?

....

....
[1]

11. Label the gland shown on this diagram of the male reproductive system.

....

What is the main hormone secreted by this gland?

....
[2]

12. What is meant by the term homeostasis?

....

....

....

....
[3]

Test 11: Homeostasis and Response

There are **12 questions** in this test. Give yourself **10 minutes** to answer them all.

1. Which of the following is an example of a coordination centre?

   A   The skin
   B   The pancreas
   C   A muscle

   [1]

2. Which is the correct pathway for stimuli along a reflex arc?

   A   relay neurone → sensory neurone → motor neurone
   B   sensory neurone → relay neurone → motor neurone

   [1]

3. How does insulin affect a person's blood sugar level?

   A   It increases it.
   B   It decreases it.

   [1]

4. Electrical impulses are used to carry information in the...

   A   ... endocrine system.
   B   ... nervous system.

   [1]

5. Which of the following is a barrier method of contraception?

   A   Contraceptive diaphragm
   B   Contraceptive patch

   [1]

6. What is reaction time?

   A   The time it takes to detect a stimulus.
   B   The time it takes to remember something.
   C   The time it takes to respond to a stimulus.

   [1]

7. How many days does the menstrual cycle usually last for?

   A   7 days
   B   28 days
   C   52 days

   [1]

8. True or False? "Hormones have longer-lasting effects than nervous impulses."

   A   True
   B   False

   [1]

Biology Paper 2: Homeostasis and Response

9. What is the role of the hormone LH in the menstrual cycle?

   ....
   [1]

10. Give two ways of controlling Type 2 diabetes.

    1. ....

    2. ....
    [2]

11. List two internal conditions that your body needs to keep constant to survive.

    1. ....

    2. ....
    [2]

12. What type of neurone transmits impulses to an effector in the nervous system?

    ....

    Give an example of an effector.

    ....
    [2]

    15

Test 12: Inheritance, Variation and Evolution

There are **12 questions** in this test. Give yourself **10 minutes** to answer them all.

1. What sex chromosomes does a biologically male human have?

   A XY

   B XXX

   C XX

   [1]

2. True or False? "Fossils can be formed from the footprints of an organism that have been preserved over time."

   A True

   B False

   [1]

3. What is a problem that could result from patients not finishing a course of antibiotics?

   A Antibiotic resistance in bacteria could increase.

   B Antibiotic resistance in bacteria could decrease.

   [1]

4. What is the correct order of classification?

   A Kingdom → Genus → Class → Order → Family → Phylum → Species

   B Kingdom → Phylum → Class → Order → Family → Genus → Species

   [1]

5. What is an organism's genotype?

   A The characteristics that the organism has.

   B The alleles that the organism has.

   [1]

6. True or False? "Selective breeding can happen without humans carrying it out."

   A True

   B False

   [1]

7. How many cell divisions occur during meiosis?

   A 1

   B 2

   C 4

   [1]

8. What type of reproduction creates clones?

   A Asexual

   B Sexual

   [1]

Biology Paper 2: Inheritance, Variation and Evolution

9. There is variation between organisms of the same species.
What is variation?

....

....
[1]

10. Describe what happens in genetic engineering.

....

....

....
[2]

11. Give two factors that might cause a species to become extinct.

1. ....

2. ....
[2]

12. The diagram on the right shows a simple evolutionary tree.
Are the whale and the shark related?

....

Explain your answer.

....

....

....
[2]

Test 13: Inheritance, Variation and Evolution

There are **12 questions** in this test. Give yourself **10 minutes** to answer them all.

1. True or False? "Some people think embryo screening is ethically wrong."
   A True
   B False
   [1]

2. What do evolutionary trees show?
   A Evolutionary relationships
   B Parental relationships
   C Genetic disorders
   [1]

3. When an individual has one dominant and one recessive allele...
   A ... the recessive allele is expressed.
   B ... the dominant allele is expressed.
   [1]

4. True or False? "The fossil record is generally accepted as good evidence for evolution."
   A True
   B False
   [1]

5. How many chromosomes does a human gamete have?
   A 12
   B 23
   C 46
   [1]

6. If a farmer wanted to increase the meat yield of his cattle, he would breed from...
   A ... the biggest cows.
   B ... the cows that produce the most milk.
   C ... those that are gentle and calm.
   [1]

7. True or False? "A mutation always has an effect on a species."
   A True
   B False
   [1]

8. True or False? "The allele for cystic fibrosis is dominant."
   A True
   B False
   [1]

Biology Paper 2: Inheritance, Variation and Evolution

9. What shape does the structure of DNA form?

   ....
   [1]

10. Give one piece of evidence that supports Darwin's theory of evolution.

    ....

    ....
    [1]

11. The allele for a tall pea plant is 'T'. The allele for a dwarf pea plant is 't'.
    A pea plant with the alleles TT is crossed with a pea plant with the alleles tt.

    The Punnett square for this cross is shown below.
    Fill in the missing squares in the Punnett square.

	t	t
T	Tt	
T		

    [2]

12. Explain how sexual reproduction produces variation.

    ....

    ....

    ....

    ....
    [3]

Test 14: Ecology

There are **13 questions** in this test. Give yourself **10 minutes** to answer them all.

1. What is an extremophile?

   A   An organism that is able to live in only one type of environment.

   B   An organism that is adapted to living in very extreme conditions.

   [1]

2. In the carbon cycle, material is broken down by...

   A   ... plants.

   B   ... microorganisms.

   C   ... animals.

   [1]

3. What type of compost should people choose to avoid contributing to global warming?

   A   Peat-free compost

   B   Compost made using peat

   [1]

4. True or False? "Photosynthesis and respiration are two processes in the water cycle."

   A   True

   B   False

   [1]

5. Which of the following factors do plants compete for?

   A   Light, space, water and mates

   B   Space, water, mineral ions and light

   [1]

6. True or False? "Global warming could reduce the Earth's biodiversity."

   A   True

   B   False

   [1]

7. What does a change in distribution of an animal mean?

   A   A change in its numbers.

   B   A change in where it lives.

   C   A change in the food it eats.

   [1]

8. Which of the following is an abiotic factor that affects animals that live in water?

   A   Oxygen level

   B   Soil pH

   C   Carbon dioxide level

   [1]

Biology Paper 2: Ecology

9. In a community, different species depend on each other for things like food or shelter. What is this called?

   ....
   [1]

10. How does respiration add to the carbon cycle?

    ....
    [1]

11. What is an adaptation?

    ....

    ....
    [1]

12. Suggest two biotic factors that can affect a community.

    1. ....

    2. ....
    [2]

13. People have set up programmes to protect ecosystems and biodiversity. Give two types of these programmes.

    1. ....

    ....

    2. ....

    ....
    [2]

Test 15: Ecology

There are **12 questions** in this test. Give yourself **10 minutes** to answer them all.

1. True or False? "When studying the distribution of an organism it is best to use a large sample size."

   A   True

   B   False

   [1]

2. What is global warming?

   A   An increase in the level of oxygen within the Earth's atmosphere.

   B   An increase in the average global temperature.

   [1]

3. Which of the following is an abiotic factor?

   A   Temperature

   B   New predators arriving

   C   New pathogens arriving

   [1]

4. Biodiversity is...

   A   ... all the organisms of one species living in a habitat.

   B   ... the variety of different species on Earth.

   [1]

5. For the human species to survive, it's important that we...

   A   ... keep increasing our standard of living.

   B   ... produce more waste.

   C   ... maintain biodiversity.

   [1]

6. A producer...

   A   ... is eaten by secondary consumers.

   B   ... makes glucose from photosynthesis.

   [1]

7. True or False? "Sewage produced by humans can pollute lakes, rivers and oceans."

   A   True

   B   False

   [1]

8. If a new predator arrives in an area, will the size of the prey population increase or decrease?

   A   Increase

   B   Decrease

   [1]

Biology Paper 2: Ecology

9. What is a stable community?

   ....

   ....
   [1]

10. Deforestation has happened on a large scale in tropical areas, like rainforest.
    Give two reasons why.

    1. ....

    2. ....
    [2]

11. Give two ways that land can become polluted by humans.

    1. ....

    2. ....
    [2]

12. Give two ways that carbon dioxide is released from peat.

    1. ....

    2. ....
    [2]

Test 16: Biology 2 Mixed Topics

There are **13 questions** in this test. Give yourself **10 minutes** to answer them all.

1. Which of these is a problem caused by the rapid rise in the world's population?

   A   Less carbon dioxide in the atmosphere.

   B   More waste is being produced.

   [1]

2. True or False? "Surgical sterilisation in males is a permanent form of contraception."

   A   True

   B   False

   [1]

3. Deforestation is...

   A   ... growing crops in forests.

   B   ... renaming forests.

   C   ... cutting down trees.

   [1]

4. Which of the following is the main reproductive hormone in men?

   A   Oestrogen

   B   Testosterone

   [1]

5. True or False? "The theory of evolution by natural selection says that all living species have evolved from simple life forms."

   A   True

   B   False

   [1]

6. What is the male gamete in plants called?

   A   Pollen

   B   Stamen

   [1]

7. What is a gene?

   A   An amino acid

   B   A small section of DNA

   [1]

8. True or False? "Some gametes are genetically identical to each other."

   A   True

   B   False

   [1]

Biology Paper 2: Mixed Topics

9. What does an effector do?

   ....

   ....
   [1]

10. Name a hormone that genetically engineered bacteria are used to make.

    ....
    [1]

11. Explain what is meant when a species is described as being 'extinct'.

    ....

    ....
    [1]

12. Name two domains of the three domain classification system.

    1. ....

    2. ....
    [2]

13. New, antibiotic-resistant strains of bacteria can quickly spread.
    Give two reasons why.

    1. ....

    ....

    2. ....

    ....
    [2]

Test 17: Biology 2 Mixed Topics

There are **12 questions** in this test. Give yourself **10 minutes** to answer them all.

1. Which one of these resources do animals compete for?

    A   Light

    B   Space

    C   Carbon dioxide

    [1]

2. True or False? "Synapses connect receptors."

    A   True

    B   False

    [1]

3. Most characteristics are controlled by...

    A   ... a single gene.

    B   ... multiple genes.

    C   ... a recessive allele.

    [1]

4. What are alleles?

    A   Different versions of the same gene.

    B   Male sex chromosomes.

    [1]

5. True or False? "We have fossil evidence of every species that ever lived."

    A   True

    B   False

    [1]

6. Who developed the three-domain classification system?

    A   Carl Linnaeus

    B   Carl Woese

    C   Charles Darwin

    [1]

7. Which type of cell division produces gametes?

    A   Meiosis

    B   Mitosis

    [1]

8. True or False? "Organisms have adaptations that allow them to survive in their own habitats."

    A   True

    B   False

    [1]

9. Alex has an X chromosome and a Y chromosome. Is Alex biologically male or female?

   ....
   [1]

10. Give two examples of a hormonal contraceptive.

    1. ....

    2. ....
    [2]

11. What is Type 2 diabetes?

    ....

    ....

    Name one risk factor for Type 2 diabetes.

    ....
    [2]

12. What is inbreeding?

    ....

    ....

    Inbreeding can lead to health problems. Explain why.

    ....

    ....
    [2]

Test 18: Atomic Structure and the Periodic Table

There are **13 questions** in this test. Give yourself **10 minutes** to answer them all.

1. True or False? "The number of protons in an atom is sometimes different to the number of neutrons."

   A True
   B False
   [1]

2. What is the name for the elements in Group 0 of the periodic table?

   A Alkali metals
   B Halogens
   C Noble gases
   [1]

3. True or False? "The further down Group 7 you go, the more reactive the elements get."

   A True
   B False
   [1]

4. What is a substance made of only one kind of atom called?

   A An element
   B A compound
   C A metal
   [1]

5. What did Niels Bohr suggest about electrons?

   A They are inside a ball of positive charge.
   B They orbit the nucleus at fixed distances.
   [1]

6. True or False? "A mixture can only be separated into its parts by breaking the chemical bonds."

   A True
   B False
   [1]

7. Most elements in the periodic table...

   A ...are non-metals.
   B ...are metals.
   [1]

8. Magnesium has 12 electrons. What is its electronic structure?

   A 6, 6
   B 8, 4
   C 2, 8, 2
   [1]

9. What do the electronic structures of elements in the same group of the periodic table have in common?

   ....
   [1]

10. How does the reactivity of Group 1 elements change as you go down the group?

    ....
    [1]

11. Complete the following to show the particles inside an atom and their relative charges.

    Particle: *Proton*   Charge: ....

    Particle: ....   Charge: *No charge*

    Particle: *Electron*   Charge: ....
    [2]

12. State what is wrong in this diagram of the electronic structure of an atom.

    ....
    [1]

13. Explain why the atoms represented on the right are isotopes. $^{12}_{6}C$ $^{14}_{6}C$

    ....

    ....
    [2]

Test 19: Bonding, Structure and Properties

There are **13 questions** in this test. Give yourself **10 minutes** to answer them all.

1. When sodium and bromine react together which element forms positive ions?

   A Sodium

   B Bromine

   [1]

2. What type of structure does silicon dioxide have?

   A Giant covalent

   B Simple molecular

   C Ionic lattice

   [1]

3. True or False? "Pure metals are harder than alloys."

   A True

   B False

   [1]

4. In which state of matter are the particles closest together?

   A Gas

   B Liquid

   C Solid

   [1]

5. What type of bond is formed when two hydrogen atoms form a molecule?

   A An ionic bond

   B A compound bond

   C A covalent bond

   [1]

6. In the following equation, what state is hydrochloric acid in?

   $Mg_{(s)} + 2HCl_{(aq)} \rightarrow MgCl_{2(aq)} + H_{2(g)}$

   A Solid

   B Gas

   C Aqueous

   [1]

7. True or False? "Ionic compounds conduct electricity when dissolved in water."

   A True

   B False

   [1]

8. What is the overall charge on an ionic compound?

   A 0

   B −1

   C +1

   [1]

Chemistry Paper 1: Bonding, Structure and Properties

9. What type of bonding is there in a Cl$_2$ molecule?

   ....
   [1]

10. Give one property of diamond.

    ....
    [1]

11. Sodium chloride is an ionic compound. What particles make up sodium chloride?

    ....

    What holds these particles together in sodium chloride?

    ....
    [2]

12. Why are polymers usually solids at room temperature?

    ....

    ....
    [1]

13. Which of the diagrams below shows a metal?

    A   B   C

    ....

    Why do metals conduct electricity?

    ....

    ....
    [2]

15

Chemistry Paper 1: Bonding, Structure and Properties

Test 20: Bonding, Structure and Properties

There are **13 questions** in this test. Give yourself **10 minutes** to answer them all.

1. What is a key feature of metallic bonding?

   A   Delocalised electrons

   B   A shared pair of electrons
   [1]

2. Why do ionic compounds have high boiling points?

   A   The bonds between the ions are weak.

   B   It takes a lot of energy to break the bonds between the ions.
   [1]

3. Giant covalent structures have...

   A   ... high melting points.

   B   ... low melting points.
   [1]

4. What does a compound made up of a metal and a non-metal consist of?

   A   Atoms

   B   Molecules

   C   Ions
   [1]

5. In a substance made up of small molecules, which of the following are stronger?

   A   The covalent bonds inside the molecules.

   B   The intermolecular forces between the molecules.
   [1]

6. Which of the following best describes the structure of diamond?

   A   Sheets of carbon atoms arranged in hexagons

   B   Giant covalent structure

   C   Giant ionic lattice
   [1]

7. True or False? "A substance made up of small molecules can conduct electricity."

   A   True

   B   False
   [1]

8. True or False? "A network of covalent bonds make graphene very strong."

   A   True

   B   False
   [1]

Chemistry Paper 1: Bonding, Structure and Properties

9. Describe how ions are formed when a metal reacts with a non-metal.

....
[1]

10. These molecules are made up of carbon atoms.
What is the name for these types of molecules?

....

Give an example of a use of these types of molecules.

....
[2]

11. Pure metals can be shaped easily.
Explain why this is in terms of the way that the atoms are arranged.

....

....
[2]

12. What kind of molecule is represented in this diagram?

....
[1]

13. Which of the substances in the table below is a gas at 90 °C?

	Melting point (°C)	Boiling point (°C)
Ethanol	−114	78
Water	0	100
Iodine	114	184

....
[1]

Test 21: Quantitative Chemistry

There are **12 questions** in this test. Give yourself **10 minutes** to answer them all.

1. What does a large range of results for an experiment mean?

   A   A small uncertainty in the results.

   B   A large uncertainty in the results.
   [1]

2. Concentration can be measured in...

   A m/s^2

   B g/dm^3

   C g/s
   [1]

3. What is the relative formula mass (M_r) of KOH?

   A   39

   B   28

   C   56
   [1]

4. True or False? "During a chemical reaction no atoms are gained or lost."

   A   True

   B   False
   [1]

5. 1 g of sodium chloride is dissolved in 2 dm^3 of water. What is the concentration of the solution?

   A   0.5 g/dm^3

   B   2 g/dm^3
   [1]

6. True or False? "In a chemical reaction, the mass of the products is always less than the mass of the reactants."

   A   True

   B   False
   [1]

7. What number should come before HCl to balance this equation?
   $Zn + \ldots HCl \rightarrow ZnCl_2 + H_2$

   A   1

   B   2

   C   3
   [1]

8. When a metal reacts fully to form a metal oxide, the mass of the metal oxide formed will be...

   A   ...greater than the mass of the metal used.

   B   ...less than the mass of the metal used.

   C   ...the same as the mass of the metal used.
   [1]

Chemistry Paper 1: Quantitative Chemistry

9. Find the relative formula mass of lithium oxide, Li_2O.

   ....

   ....

   ....
   [2]

10. An experiment measuring the volume of gas given off during a reaction was repeated five times. The results are shown below.

Experiment 1	Experiment 2	Experiment 3	Experiment 4	Experiment 5
12 cm³	9 cm³	13 cm³	12 cm³	10 cm³

    Find the range of the results.

    ....

    ....
    [1]

11. Aluminium can be extracted from aluminium oxide via electrolysis. Balance the equation for the reaction.

    $$..... Al_2O_{3(l)} \rightarrow ..... Al_{(l)} + ... O_{2(g)}$$
    [2]

12. What mass of NaOH should be dissolved in 0.50 dm³ of water to make a solution with a concentration of 0.50 g/dm³?

    ....

    ....

    ....

    .... g
    [2]

Test 22: Chemical Changes

There are **12 questions** in this test. Give yourself **10 minutes** to answer them all.

1. What does a pH of 7 indicate?

   A   An acidic solution

   B   An alkaline solution

   C   A neutral solution

   [1]

2. True or False? "An insoluble base will react with an acid."

   A   True

   B   False

   [1]

3. True or False? "Hydrochloric acid and magnesium react to produce magnesium chloride and hydrogen."

   A   True

   B   False

   [1]

4. An alkaline solution of potassium hydroxide reacts with nitric acid to produce...

   A   ... carbon dioxide and water.

   B   ... a salt and water.

   [1]

5. Iron reacts with oxygen to form iron oxide. What type of reaction is this?

   A   Oxidation reaction

   B   Reduction reaction

   C   Neutralisation reaction

   [1]

6. True or False? "Metals below carbon in the reactivity series can be extracted from their ore by reduction using carbon."

   A   True

   B   False

   [1]

7. True or False? "All metals are found in the ground as ores."

   A   True

   B   False

   [1]

8. How can a solid salt be obtained from a salt solution?

   A   By adding an indicator.

   B   By adding a catalyst.

   C   By crystallisation of the salt solution.

   [1]

Chemistry Paper 1: Chemical Changes

9. Name the two gases formed in the electrolysis of sodium chloride solution.

   1. ....

   2. ....
   [2]

10. Magnesium and iron both react with dilute hydrochloric acid.
    Describe how the reactions differ in terms of reactivity. Give a reason for the difference.

    ....

    ....
    [2]

11. Why can't ionic solids be electrolysed?

    ....

    ....
    [1]

12. Name a metal that is extracted from its ore using electrolysis.

    ....

    Explain why this metal is extracted this way.

    ....

    ....
    [2]

Test 23: Energy Changes

There are **12 questions** in this test. Give yourself **10 minutes** to answer them all.

1. True or False? "Energy is conserved in all chemical reactions."

   A True

   B False

   [1]

2. If a reaction gives out energy to the surroundings, the products of the reaction have...

   A ...more energy than the reactants.

   B ...less energy than the reactants.

   [1]

3. If the surroundings increase in temperature during a reaction...

   A ...the reaction is endothermic.

   B ...the reaction is exothermic.

   [1]

4. Is the reaction between citric acid and sodium hydrogencarbonate exothermic or endothermic?

   A Exothermic

   B Endothermic

   [1]

5. In an endothermic reaction, the products are at...

   A ...a lower energy than the reactants.

   B ...a higher energy than the reactants.

   [1]

6. Which of these uses an endothermic reaction?

   A Self-heating drinks can

   B Some sports injury packs

   [1]

7. What is the activation energy of a reaction?

   A The maximum amount of energy needed by the particles to react.

   B The minimum amount of energy needed by the particles to react.

   [1]

8. Which of the following can be used to measure the energy change when a chemical reaction occurs?

   A Change in colour

   B Change in temperature

   [1]

Chemistry Paper 1: Energy Changes

9. Not every collision between reacting particles results in a reaction. Explain why this is.

....

.... [1]

10. Why do hand warmers use exothermic reactions and not endothermic reactions?

....

.... [1]

11. Give an example of a type of reaction that is exothermic.

.... [1]

12. Does this energy level diagram show an exothermic or an endothermic reaction? Explain your answer.

....

....

....

Which arrow (A, B, C or D) represents the overall energy change of the reaction?

....

Which arrow (A, B, C or D) represents the activation energy of the reaction?

.... [4]

Test 24: Chemistry 1 Mixed Topics

There are **12 questions** in this test. Give yourself **10 minutes** to answer them all.

1. True or False? "Atoms of the same element all have the same number of neutrons."

   A True
   B False
   [1]

2. When carbonates react with dilute acid they produce...

   A ...carbon dioxide.
   B ...hydrogen.
   C ...oxygen.
   [1]

3. Which of the following would you expect to have the lowest boiling point?

   A A giant ionic structure
   B A substance consisting of small molecules
   C A giant covalent structure
   [1]

4. How are the elements arranged in the modern periodic table?

   A In order of atomic number.
   B In order of atomic mass.
   C In the order that they were discovered.
   [1]

5. Metal oxides are...

   A ...acids
   B ...bases
   [1]

6. What is an exothermic reaction?

   A A reaction which transfers energy to the surroundings.
   B A reaction which takes in energy from the surroundings.
   [1]

7. True or False? "When forming an ionic bond, metal atoms lose electrons to form positive ions."

   A True
   B False
   [1]

8. What type of compounds are formed when alkali metals react with non-metals?

   A Covalent compounds
   B Ionic compounds
   [1]

Chemistry Paper 1: Mixed Topics

9. Name the type of structure shown in the diagram:

....
[1]

10. Metal A displaces metal B from an aqueous solution of its salt.
    What does this tell you about metals A and B?

....

....
[1]

11. State the two products formed in a reaction between a metal and an acid.

   1. ....

   2. ....
[2]

12. According to the law of conservation of mass, how does the mass
    of the products of a reaction compare to the mass of the reactants?

....

....

A sample of copper carbonate was strongly heated in an open beaker.
The equation below shows the thermal decomposition reaction that took place.

$$CuCO_{3(s)} \xrightarrow{heat} CO_{2(g)} + CuO_{(s)}$$

The mass of the beaker and its contents was measured before and after heating.
Explain why the mass was lower after heating than before heating.

....

....
[3]

15

Test 25: Chemistry 1 Mixed Topics

There are **13 questions** in this test. Give yourself **10 minutes** to answer them all.

1. An atom has a mass number of 23 and an atomic number of 11. How many neutrons does it have?

    A 11
    B 12
    C 23
    [1]

2. What name is given to the total number of protons and neutrons in an atom?

    A Electronic structure
    B Atomic number
    C Mass number
    [1]

3. Beryllium is in Group 2 of the periodic table. What is the charge on a beryllium ion?

    A 2+
    B 1+
    C 2−
    [1]

4. True or False? "All covalent substances have a giant covalent structure."

    A True
    B False
    [1]

5. True or False? "The discovery of the electron led to the plum pudding atomic model."

    A True
    B False
    [1]

6. True or False? "Pure metals can be bent because the layers of atoms can slide over each other."

    A True
    B False
    [1]

7. Which of these is an endothermic reaction?

    A Combustion
    B Thermal decomposition
    [1]

8. What happens to the boiling points of the elements as you go down Group 0?

    A They decrease.
    B They increase.
    C They remain fairly constant.
    [1]

Chemistry Paper 1: Mixed Topics

9. Chlorine gas is bubbled through a solution of potassium bromide.
The equation for this reaction is shown below.

$$Cl_2 + 2KBr \rightarrow Br_2 + 2KCl$$

Why does this reaction occur?

....

What would happen if bromine vapour was bubbled through potassium chloride solution?

....
[2]

10. When molten lead bromide is electrolysed, which electrode is lead produced at?

....
[1]

11. An element has the electronic structure 2, 8, 4.
Which group of the periodic table must it be in? Explain your answer.

....

....
[2]

12. State the relative masses of protons, neutrons and electrons in an atom.

proton: .... neutron: .... electron: ....
[1]

13. What does the pH tell you about a substance?

....

....
[1]

15

Chemistry Paper 2

Test 26: Rate and Extent of Chemical Change

There are **11 questions** in this test. Give yourself **10 minutes** to answer them all.

1. How does a catalyst increase a reaction's rate?

   A It increases the energy of the reactants.

   B It provides a different pathway for the reaction that has a lower activation energy.
   [1]

2. Which of these reactions would be faster?

   A Magnesium with concentrated hydrochloric acid

   B Magnesium with dilute hydrochloric acid
   [1]

3. When a reversible reaction occurs in a sealed reaction vessel, when is equilibrium reached?

   A When the amounts of products and reactants are equal.

   B When the rates of the forward and reverse reactions are equal.
   [1]

4. True or False? "The mean rate of reaction can be found by measuring the amount of reactant used over a period of time."

   A True

   B False
   [1]

5. The rate of a reaction doesn't depend on the...

   A ... frequency of collisions.

   B ... volume of solution.

   C ... temperature of the reactants.
   [1]

6. True or False? "A reversible reaction can take in energy in both directions."

   A True

   B False
   [1]

7. Increasing the concentration of a reactant in a solution means that the solution...

   A ... contains more reactant particles.

   B ... contains fewer reactant particles.
   [1]

8. Which of the following is not a unit of reaction rate?

   A g/s

   B cm^3/s

   C g/dm^3
   [1]

9. Sodium carbonate and hydrochloric acid are reacted together and the gas produced is collected in a gas syringe. 30 cm³ of gas is collected over 12 seconds.

What formula should you use to calculate the mean rate of this reaction?

....

....

Calculate the mean rate of the reaction. Include the correct units in your answer.

....

....
[3]

10. The diagram shows the results of the same reaction carried out in two different experiments.

Was the rate of reaction greater in Experiment 1 or Experiment 2?

....

Suggest one way in which the conditions may have been changed in Experiment 2.

....
[2]

11. Breaking a solid reactant up into smaller pieces increases the rate of a reaction. Use collision theory to explain why this is.

....

....

....
[2]

Test 27: Rate and Extent of Chemical Change

There are **12 questions** in this test. Give yourself **10 minutes** to answer them all.

1. What is a reversible reaction?

   A A reaction where the products of the reaction can react to produce further products.

   B A reaction where the products of the reaction can react to produce the original reactants.

   [1]

2. Which of the following is a reason why increasing the temperature increases the rate of a reaction?

   A The reactant particles stick together more.

   B The reactant particles move faster so they collide more frequently.

   [1]

3. True or False? "Different catalysts are needed for different reactions."

   A True

   B False

   [1]

4. In a reaction between marble and hydrochloric acid, using small marble chips instead of a large piece of marble will produce...

   A ... no difference in the rate of reaction.

   B ... a faster rate of reaction.

   C ... a slower rate of reaction.

   [1]

5. Which of the following can be measured to determine the rate of a reaction?

   A Change in temperature.

   B Volume of gas produced.

   [1]

6. True or False? "Collision theory says that the more particles that collide in a reaction, the hotter the reaction gets."

   A True

   B False

   [1]

7. Which of the following makes the collisions between particles more energetic?

   A Increasing the gas pressure.

   B Increasing the temperature.

   [1]

8. Halving the frequency of collisions in a reaction mixture...

   A ... halves the reaction rate.

   B ... doubles the reaction rate.

   [1]

Chemistry Paper 2: Rate and Extent of Chemical Change

9. A reversible reaction is often said to be at equilibrium. What is meant by this?

....

....
[1]

10. The equation for the decomposition of hydrogen peroxide is shown below:

$$2H_2O_{2(aq)} \rightarrow 2H_2O_{(l)} + O_{2(g)}$$

How would you expect the total volume of O_2 produced to be affected by the presence of a catalyst? Explain your answer.

....

....

....
[2]

11. Use collision theory to explain why increasing the pressure of reacting gases increases the rate of a reaction.

....

....

....
[2]

12. Calcium and water are reacted with each other in a beaker placed on a mass balance.
At the start of the reaction the mass balance reads 150 g.
After 40 seconds the mass balance reads 147 g.
Calculate the mean rate of reaction during this time.

....

....

....

.... g/s
[2]

15

Test 28: Organic Chemistry

There are **12 questions** in this test. Give yourself **10 minutes** to answer them all.

1. Crude oil is a...

   A ...renewable resource.

   B ...finite resource.

   C ...infinite resource.
   [1]

2. What is the general formula of an alkane?

   A C_nH_{2n}

   B C_nH_{2n+2}
   [1]

3. True or False? "Alkenes are more reactive than alkanes."

   A True

   B False
   [1]

4. Why are longer hydrocarbons often cracked to make shorter ones?

   A To make more useful hydrocarbons.

   B To make less flammable hydrocarbons.

   C To make products like tar.
   [1]

5. True or False? "The shorter the hydrocarbon, the more viscous it is."

   A True

   B False
   [1]

6. What happens to the carbon and hydrogen in a fuel when it's burned?

   A They are oxidised.

   B They evaporate.

   C They react to form CH_4.
   [1]

7. Which technique is used to separate the components of crude oil?

   A Cracking

   B Filtration

   C Fractional distillation
   [1]

8. Which of the methods below could be used to crack a long chain hydrocarbon?

   A Mix the hydrocarbon with water and add a cold platinum catalyst.

   B Mix the hydrocarbon vapour with steam and heat to a very high temperature.
   [1]

9. Draw the alkane with the formula C₂H₆, showing all the bonds present.

What is the name of this alkane?

....
[2]

10. Complete the word equation below for the complete combustion of propane:

propane + oxygen → .... + water
[1]

11. The formulas of two alkanes, decane and pentane, are shown below:

Decane: C₁₀H₂₂

Pentane: C₅H₁₂

Which of these alkanes will have the higher boiling point?
Explain your answer.

....

....
[2]

12. What substance is used to test for alkenes?

....

What would you observe if an alkene is present?

....
[2]

Test 29: Chemical Analysis

There are **12 questions** in this test. Give yourself **10 minutes** to answer them all.

1. What is the test for hydrogen?

   A   It burns with a green flame.

   B   It turns damp litmus paper white.

   C   It burns with a pop.
   [1]

2. When carbon dioxide is bubbled through limewater, the limewater turns...

   A   ...cloudy.

   B   ...green.

   C   ...yellow.
   [1]

3. True or False? "During paper chromatography, the paper must remain fully submerged in solvent."

   A   True

   B   False
   [1]

4. True or False? "Formulations are made for a specific purpose by mixing together exact amounts of different components."

   A   True

   B   False
   [1]

5. You can check if a substance is pure by...

   A   ...testing its melting point.

   B   ...using universal indicator solution.

   C   ...shaking it with limewater.
   [1]

6. In chemistry, what is a pure substance?

   A   Any substance in its natural state

   B   A substance that only contains one compound or element.
   [1]

7. True or False? "Oxygen will relight a glowing splint."

   A   True

   B   False
   [1]

8. How many different phases are used in chromatography?

   A   1

   B   2

   C   3
   [1]

9. Describe the chemical test for chlorine gas.

   ....

   .... [1]

10. The melting point of pure water is 0 °C.
    The melting point of a sample of water is −2 °C. Suggest why this is.

    .... [1]

11. A student carries out paper chromatography on a substance.
    The solvent travelled 5.0 cm up the chromatography paper.
    The substance left a single spot 3.2 cm up the chromatography paper.

    What is the formula for calculating an R_f value?

    ....

    ....

    What is the R_f value of the substance?

    ....

    .... [2]

12. Name the phases involved in chromatography.

    ....

    Explain how the pattern of spots produced in a chromatography experiment
    can be used to distinguish a pure substance from an impure substance.

    ....

    ....

    .... [3]

Test 30: Chemistry of the Atmosphere

There are **11 questions** in this test. Give yourself **10 minutes** to answer them all.

1. Why is sulfur often removed from fuels before they are burnt?

    A So the fuel produces less soot when it burns.

    B To reduce the cost of the fuel.

    C To reduce acid rain.
    [1]

2. Which of these is not produced when a fuel undergoes complete combustion?

    A Carbon monoxide

    B Carbon dioxide

    C Water
    [1]

3. Which of these is causing the average global temperature to rise?

    A An increasing amount of greenhouse gases in the atmosphere.

    B An increased amount of particulates in the atmosphere from car exhausts.
    [1]

4. It is difficult for scientists to be certain what the implications of global climate change will be because...

    A ...the evidence has not been peer-reviewed.

    B ...the Earth's climate is very complicated so is hard to model.
    [1]

5. True or False? "Nitrogen oxides form when fuels burn slowly at low temperatures."

    A True

    B False
    [1]

6. Which of the following is formed mainly from shells and skeletons of marine organisms?

    A Limestone

    B Coal
    [1]

7. Which of these gases is not a greenhouse gas?

    A Water vapour

    B Methane

    C Oxygen
    [1]

8. What percentage of the Earth's atmosphere is made up of oxygen?

    A About 80%

    B About 20%

    C Less than 1%
    [1]

Chemistry Paper 2: Chemistry of the Atmosphere

9. Algae were the first producers of a gas that is now in the atmosphere. Name this gas.

   ....

   Name the process through which algae produced this gas.

   ....
   [2]

10. Rising global temperatures may lead to the polar ice caps melting.
    State one environmental implication of this.

    ....

    ....

    Briefly describe two other potential effects of rising global temperatures.

    1. ....

    ....

    2. ....

    ....
    [3]

11. Give two human activities that increase the amount of carbon dioxide in the atmosphere.

    1. ....

    ....

    2. ....

    ....
    [2]

Test 31: Chemistry of the Atmosphere

There are **11 questions** in this test. Give yourself **10 minutes** to answer them all.

1. True or False? "Greenhouse gases in the atmosphere help to keep temperatures on Earth high enough to support life."

   A   True

   B   False

   [1]

2. Which of these gases makes up the smallest proportion of our atmosphere?

   A   Oxygen

   B   Nitrogen

   C   Carbon dioxide

   [1]

3. True or False? "We can reduce the carbon footprint of the power we use by using nuclear energy instead of fossil fuels."

   A   True

   B   False

   [1]

4. Solid particles in the atmosphere block some sunlight from reaching the Earth's surface. What is this effect called?

   A   Global warming

   B   Global dimming

   [1]

5. Carbon monoxide is...

   A   ...a toxic gas.

   B   ...a hydrocarbon.

   C   ...a cause of acid rain.

   [1]

6. Which of these gases can cause respiratory problems?

   A   Sulfur dioxide

   B   Nitrogen

   C   Carbon Dioxide

   [1]

7. Which of the following is a reason why carbon dioxide levels decreased in the Earth's early atmosphere?

   A   Sedimentary rocks and fossil fuels containing carbon formed.

   B   The carbon dioxide reacted with oxygen in the atmosphere.

   [1]

8. Greenhouse gases...

   A   ...absorb short wavelength radiation from the Sun.

   B   ...absorb long wavelength radiation from the Earth.

   [1]

Chemistry Paper 2: Chemistry of the Atmosphere

9. Which gas made up most of the Earth's early atmosphere?

   ....

   Name two other gases present in the Earth's early atmosphere.

   1. .... 2. ....

   Where did these gases come from?

   ....
   [3]

10. Describe one way that governments can reduce carbon dioxide emissions.

    ....

    ....

    Give one reason why the actions of governments are limited.

    ....

    ....
    [2]

11. Give two human activities that increase the amount of methane in the atmosphere.

    1. ....

    2. ....
    [2]

Test 32: Using Resources

There are **11 questions** in this test. Give yourself **10 minutes** to answer them all.

1. What do life cycle assessments look at?

   A The total environmental cost of a product.

   B The economic impact of a product.
   [1]

2. Which process produces sewage sludge and effluent during sewage treatment?

   A Screening

   B Aerobic biological treatment

   C Sedimentation
   [1]

3. Potable water is...

   A ...water that is pure.

   B ...water that is safe to drink.

   C ...ground water.
   [1]

4. Producing potable water from seawater...

   A ...is not possible.

   B ...requires a lot of energy.

   C ...is the method used in the UK.
   [1]

5. True or False? "Life cycle assessments are free from bias."

   A True

   B False
   [1]

6. True or False? "Metals can be recycled but glass cannot be."

   A True

   B False
   [1]

7. True or False? "Potable water must contain no dissolved salts."

   A True

   B False
   [1]

8. Which of the following is an example of a renewable resource?

   A Copper

   B Wool

   C Nuclear fuel such as uranium
   [1]

9. Describe one environmental impact of obtaining raw materials from the Earth.

....

....
[1]

10. Potable water can be produced from fresh water. This process involves sterilising the water to kill any harmful bacteria or microbes.
Give two ways in which water can be sterilised.

1. ....

2. ....
[2]

11. What are the four stages of a product's life that are examined during a life cycle assessment?

1. ....

2. ....

3. ....

4. ....
[4]

Test 33: Chemistry 2 Mixed Topics

There are **13 questions** in this test. Give yourself **10 minutes** to answer them all.

1. True or False? "Oxygen is the most abundant gas in the atmosphere."

   A True
   B False
   [1]

2. How many hydrogen atoms does ethane contain?

   A 2
   B 6
   C 8
   [1]

3. On a graph showing the quantity of product formed against time, a tangent to the curve gives the...

   A ...concentration of the product.
   B ...rate of reaction at a specific time.
   [1]

4. Which of these effects on the planet is associated with burning fossil fuels?

   A An increase in the average global temperature.
   B An increase in the amount of oxygen in the oceans.
   [1]

5. Which of these processes can be used to desalinate sea water?

   A Sterilisation
   B Reverse osmosis
   C Sedimentation
   [1]

6. True or False? "Chemical reactions all happen at the same rate."

   A True
   B False
   [1]

7. True or False? "Increasing the pressure of any reaction mixture will increase the reaction rate."

   A True
   B False
   [1]

8. True or False? "Taxing companies based on the amount of greenhouse gases they produce aims to increase the country's carbon footprint."

   A True
   B False
   [1]

Chemistry Paper 2: Mixed Topics

9. What is meant by the carbon footprint of a product?

   ....

   ....

   ....
   [2]

10. Describe two reasons why increasing temperature leads to an increase in the rate of reaction.

    1. ....

    2. ....
    [2]

11. Many different fertilisers can be described as a "formulation". What does this mean?

    ....

    ....
    [1]

12. Describe the chemical test for oxygen.

    ....

    ....
    [1]

13. Give one benefit of recycling metals.

    ....

    ....
    [1]

Test 34: Chemistry 2 Mixed Topics

There are **12 questions** in this test. Give yourself **10 minutes** to answer them all.

1. What is the first stage in making fresh water safe to drink?

   A Filtration
   B Distillation
   C Sterilisation
   [1]

2. Why can hydrocarbons of different lengths be separated by fractional distillation?

   A They have different boiling points.
   B They have different melting points.
   C They have different viscosities.
   [1]

3. True or False? "Changes in the Earth's climate may mean certain regions struggle to produce food."

   A True
   B False
   [1]

4. Which of the following cannot be used to show that a sample of a substance is impure?

   A Melting or boiling point data.
   B Chromatography.
   C Crystallisation.
   [1]

5. True or False? "In chromatography, the R_f value for a substance will be the same no matter what solvent is used."

   A True
   B False
   [1]

6. If a reversible reaction is endothermic in one direction, what will it be in the other direction?

   A Endothermic
   B Could be exothermic or endothermic.
   C Exothermic
   [1]

7. True or False? "Catalysts are used up during a reaction."

   A True
   B False
   [1]

8. True or False? "Companies sometimes use biased life cycle assessments to support their own products."

   A True
   B False
   [1]

9. A certain reaction is carried out with and without a catalyst.

Which line on the reaction profile shows the reaction with a catalyst? Explain your answer.

....

.... *[2]*

10. Describe the chemical test for carbon dioxide.

....

.... *[1]*

11. A process used in sewage treatment separates sewage into effluent and sludge. Name this process.

....

What process is used to break down the sludge?

.... *[2]*

12. Give two reasons why the levels of carbon dioxide in the early atmosphere of Earth began to decrease.

1. ....

....

2. ....

.... *[2]*

Test 35: Energy

There are **12 questions** in this test. Give yourself **10 minutes** to answer them all.

1. What happens to the amount of energy in a car's kinetic energy store when the car slows down?

   A   It stays the same.

   B   It decreases.

   [1]

2. Which of the following would decrease the rate of cooling of a garage?

   A   Decreasing the thickness of its walls.

   B   Increasing the thickness of its walls.

   [1]

3. When an apple falls from a tree, energy is transferred...

   A   ... away from its gravitational potential energy store.

   B   ... to its gravitational potential energy store.

   [1]

4. Which of these is a disadvantage of using wind turbines to generate electricity?

   A   They produce dangerous waste that is difficult to dispose of.

   B   They release atmospheric pollution (CO_2) when running.

   C   They can be noisy.

   [1]

5. The amount of energy transferred by an appliance depends on...

   A   ... its power and size.

   B   ... its power and the time it is on for.

   [1]

6. 4 J of energy is supplied to a device with an efficiency of 50%. What is the useful output energy transfer of the device?

   A   2 J

   B   4 J

   C   6 J

   [1]

7. When a racket hits a ball, energy is transferred from the racket's kinetic energy store to the ball's kinetic energy store. This energy is transferred...

   A   ... by heating.

   B   ... mechanically.

   [1]

8. Two materials are cooled by 10° C. They have the same mass and different specific heat capacities. Which material emits more energy?

   A   The material with the higher specific heat capacity

   B   The material with the lower specific heat capacity

   [1]

Physics Paper 1: Energy

9. Name two types of fossil fuel.

1. ....

2. ....
[2]

10. State one problem with generating electricity using nuclear power.

....

....
[1]

11. A go-kart travels along a straight track at 10 m/s. The go-kart and its driver have a combined mass of 160 kg. The equation below gives the energy in the kinetic energy store of a moving object.

$$\text{kinetic energy} = 0.5 \times \text{mass} \times (\text{speed})^2$$

Calculate the total energy in the kinetic energy stores of the go-kart and driver.

....

....

Energy = ... J
[2]

12. Substance X has a specific heat capacity of 400 J/kg°C.

Calculate the amount of energy needed to increase the temperature of 0.5 kg of substance X by 15 °C.

change in thermal energy = mass × specific heat capacity × temperature change

....

....

....

Energy = ... J
[2]

Physics Paper 1: Energy

Test 36: Energy

There are **12 questions** in this test. Give yourself **10 minutes** to answer them all.

1. Power is the...

   A   ... energy of a moving object.

   B   ... rate of doing work.

   [1]

2. When a spring is compressed, which of these energy stores is energy transferred to?

   A   The spring's elastic potential energy store

   B   The spring's nuclear energy store

   [1]

3. What is the name of a system in which there is no net change in the total energy?

   A   A closed system

   B   An open system

   C   A mechanical system

   [1]

4. Electric heater A has a power rating of 1 kW. Electric heater B has a power rating of 880 W. Which transfers the most energy in 2 hours?

   A   Heater A

   B   Heater B

   [1]

5. The rate of energy transfer from a house can be reduced by...

   A   ... having walls with a low thermal conductivity.

   B   ... having walls with a high thermal conductivity.

   [1]

6. Pick a suitable option that can be used to reduce unwanted energy transfers in a battery-powered toy car.

   A   Insulate the car.

   B   Increase the input energy to the car.

   C   Lubricate any moving parts in the car.

   [1]

7. Which of the following is a possible reason for why we continue to use non-renewable resources?

   A   Because non-renewable resources will never run out.

   B   Because non-renewable resources are more reliable than renewable alternatives.

   [1]

8. A cannon uses explosives to launch a ball into the air. Which is a wasteful energy transfer that occurs when the cannon is fired?

   A   Chemical energy store of explosives → Kinetic energy store of ball

   B   Chemical energy store of explosives → Thermal energy store of ball

   [1]

Physics Paper 1: Energy

9. Give one example of a renewable energy resource.

....

[1]

10. A student uses a heater to provide energy to two 0.5 kg blocks made from different materials. He measures their temperatures at regular intervals for five minutes. The graph on the right shows his results. State and explain which block of material has the highest specific heat capacity.

....

....

[2]

11. Describe the useful energy transfers in a hairdryer.

....

....

....

[2]

12. A 0.5 kg object is sat at the top of a 30 m high cliff. The equation below relates the amount of energy in an object's gravitational potential energy store to its mass, the gravitational field strength and the height of the object.

Gravitational potential energy = mass × gravitational field strength × height

If the gravitational field strength, $g = 9.8$ N/kg, calculate the energy in the object's gravitational potential energy store.

....

....

....

Energy = ... J

[2]

15

Test 37: Electricity

There are **12 questions** in this test. Give yourself **10 minutes** to answer them all.

1. Which of the following is a device that emits light?

   A Fuse
   B LDR
   C LED
   [1]

2. True or False? "The current is the same at any point in a single closed loop of wire that is connected to a power supply".

   A True
   B False
   [1]

3. In the UK, what is the typical potential difference between the live wire and earth wire in an electrical appliance?

   A 230 V
   B 12 V
   C 0 V
   [1]

4. The purpose of the earth wire in an appliance is...

   A ... to carry the alternating potential difference from the supply.
   B ... to carry the alternating potential difference away from the appliance.
   C ... to stop the appliance becoming live.
   [1]

5. True or False? "Two components connected in parallel will each have the same potential difference across them."

   A True
   B False
   [1]

6. True or False? "The UK mains electricity supply is direct current."

   A True
   B False
   [1]

7. True or False? "In a series circuit, the power supply's potential difference is shared between all components."

   A True
   B False
   [1]

8. True or False? "Step-up transformers are used to increase the potential difference of electricity."

   A True
   B False
   [1]

Physics Paper 1: Electricity

9. While in use, a 1.2 V cell transfers 5400 J of energy. The equation below shows the relationship between charge flow, energy transferred and potential difference.

charge flow = energy transferred ÷ potential difference

How much charge passed through the cell while it was in use?

....

....

Charge = ... C

[2]

10. A student is investigating the relationship between the length of a conductor and its resistance.

The graph on the right shows the results of her experiment.

Describe the relationship between the length of the conductor and its resistance.

....

....

[1]

11. A current of 3.0 A passes through a resistor with a resistance of 10 Ω. Calculate the potential difference across the resistor.

....

....

Potential difference = ... V

[3]

12. Name the circuit component shown on the right.

....

[1]

Physics Paper 1: Electricity

Test 38: Electricity

There are **12 questions** in this test. Give yourself **10 minutes** to answer them all.

1. True or False? "The resistance of a thermistor is higher in hot conditions than in the cold."
   A True
   B False
   [1]

2. What type of resistor can be used in lights that turn on automatically when it gets dark?
   A Thermistor
   B LDR
   [1]

3. What is the name for electric current that is constantly changing direction?
   A Alternating current (ac)
   B Direct current (dc)
   C Switching current (sc)
   [1]

4. The resistance of an ohmic conductor at a constant temperature...
   A ... increases with current.
   B ... doesn't change with current.
   [1]

5. In a circuit with a fixed potential difference, what would happen to the current if you increased the resistance?
   A The current would stay the same.
   B The current would decrease.
   [1]

6. When two resistors are connected in parallel, their combined resistance is...
   A ... lower than it would be if they were connected in series.
   B ... higher than it would be if they were connected in series.
   C ... the same as it would be if they were connected in series.
   [1]

7. Electric current is...
   A ... the driving force that pushes charges around a circuit.
   B ... the flow of electrical charge.
   [1]

8. Which wire inside a three-core cable is coated with blue plastic?
   A Earth
   B Live
   C Neutral
   [1]

Physics Paper 1: Electricity

9. The image below shows the national grid.

State the name given to the electrical devices labelled X.

....
[1]

10. State the frequency and potential difference of the UK mains supply.

Frequency = ... Hz   Potential difference = ... V
[2]

11. The circuit diagram below shows two resistors connected in series with a battery.
Find the reading on voltmeter V_3.

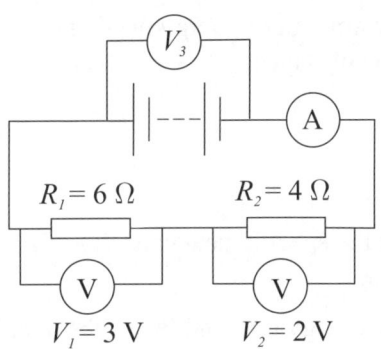

....

Potential difference = ... V

Find the total resistance, R, of the circuit.

....

Resistance = ... Ω
[2]

12. Hair straighteners with a power of 57.5 W are plugged into a 230 V mains supply. The equation below shows the relationship between power, potential difference and current.

current = power ÷ potential difference

Calculate the current through the hair straighteners.

....

....

Current = ... A
[2]

15

Test 39: Particle Model of Matter

There are **13 questions** in this test. Give yourself **10 minutes** to answer them all.

1. True or False? "Liquids are generally denser than solids."

   A True

   B False

   [1]

2. True or False? "The temperature of a gas is related to the average energy in the kinetic energy stores of its particles."

   A True

   B False

   [1]

3. What is the specific latent heat of fusion?

   A The amount of energy needed to melt 1 kg of a substance.

   B The amount of energy needed to boil 1 kg of a substance.

   [1]

4. The internal energy of a system is equal to...

   A ... the total energy that its particles have in their kinetic energy stores.

   B ... the total energy that its particles have in their kinetic and potential energy stores.

   [1]

5. What is the specific heat capacity of a substance?

   A The energy released by a substance when it freezes.

   B The energy needed to raise the temperature of 1 kg of a substance by 1°C.

   [1]

6. True or False? "Changes of state are physical changes."

   A True

   B False

   [1]

7. What happens to the mass of a substance when it changes from a solid to a liquid?

   A It increases

   B It decreases

   C It stays the same

   [1]

8. What will happen to the pressure of a fixed volume of gas if its temperature is increased?

   A It will decrease

   B It will increase

   [1]

Physics Paper 1: Particle Model of Matter

9. State the units for specific latent heat.

....
[1]

10. Describe how the arrangement of particles in a solid is different to the arrangement of particles in a gas.

....

....
[1]

11. A temperature-time graph for a substance that is being cooled down is shown on the right. Identify the state of the substance at point X.

State = ...
[1]

12. A piece of gold has a volume of 2.00×10^{-5} m³ and a mass of 0.386 kg. Density, mass and volume are related by the equation below.

$$\text{density} = \text{mass} \div \text{volume}$$

Calculate the density of gold.

....

....

Density = ... kg/m³
[2]

13. Describe how the density of a regular solid cube can be measured.

....

....

....
[2]

Test 40: Atomic Structure

There are **12 questions** in this test. Give yourself **10 minutes** to answer them all.

1. What is the name for atoms with the same number of protons but different numbers of neutrons?

   A Ions

   B Isotopes

   [1]

2. True or False? "The results of the alpha scattering experiment led to the development of the plum pudding model of the atom."

   A True

   B False

   [1]

3. The count rate of a radioactive sample falls from 130 Bq to 65 Bq in 15 minutes. What is its half-life?

   A 15 minutes

   B 30 minutes

   C 1 hour

   [1]

4. True or False? "Living cells can be damaged by ionising radiation."

   A True

   B False

   [1]

5. What happens to the atomic number of a radioactive nucleus when it emits an alpha particle?

   A It increases

   B It decreases

   [1]

6. Which type of radiation can penetrate the furthest into materials?

   A Alpha

   B Beta

   C Gamma

   [1]

7. Which type of radiation is the same as an electron?

   A Alpha

   B Beta

   C Gamma

   [1]

8. Which of the following gives the number of neutrons in the nucleus of an atom?

   A The mass number

   B The mass number − the atomic number

   C The mass number + the atomic number

   [1]

Physics Paper 1: Atomic Structure

9. What is the difference between an atom and an ion?

....

....
[1]

10. The graph on the right shows the number of radioactive nuclei in a sample over time. Use the graph to calculate how long it would take for the number of radioactive nuclei in the sample to fall to one quarter of its initial amount.

....

....

....

Time = ... years
[3]

11. An electron is in orbit around an atom's nucleus. The electron absorbs an electromagnetic wave. What happens to the electron's orbit?

....
[1]

12. Describe the difference between irradiation and contamination.

....

....

....
[2]

Test 41: Physics 1 Mixed Topics

There are **12 questions** in this test. Give yourself **10 minutes** to answer them all.

1. What happens to the resistance of a filament lamp as the temperature of the filament increases?

   A   It increases

   B   It decreases

   [1]

2. True or False? "Transformers are used to carry electricity all around the country."

   A   True

   B   False

   [1]

3. Which of the following changes in state is called 'sublimation'?

   A   gas to liquid

   B   solid to gas

   C   solid to liquid

   [1]

4. Which of the following equations shows the correct relationship between the power of a device (P), its resistance (R) and the current flowing through it (I)?

   A $P = IR$

   B $P = IR^2$

   C $P = I^2R$

   [1]

5. What is the power of a device that transfers 20 J in 2 s?

   A   10 W

   B   40 W

   [1]

6. True or False? "If a resistor is added to a circuit in parallel, the total resistance of the circuit will increase."

   A   True

   B   False

   [1]

7. True or False? "Biofuels are made over millions of years from dead organic material."

   A   True

   B   False

   [1]

8. Which of these is true in the nuclear model of the atom?

   A   The mass of the atom is concentrated at its centre.

   B   The nucleus in the atom is uncharged.

   [1]

Physics Paper 1: Mixed Topics

9. What happens to the average energy of the particles in a system when the system is heated?

   ....

   [1]

10. A sample contains 1.2×10^5 radioactive nuclei of isotope Y.
    How many nuclei of isotope Y will there be after one half-life?

    ....

    Number of nuclei = ...
    [1]

11. The equation below shows the alpha decay of an isotope of americium. Complete the equation by writing the missing atomic number and mass number of the product.

    $$^{241}_{95}Am \rightarrow \,^{\ldots}_{\ldots}Np + \,^{4}_{2}He$$
    [2]

12. A spring is extended by 0.03 m, causing 0.9 J to be stored in its elastic potential energy store. The equation below shows the relationship between the elastic potential energy, the spring constant and the extension of a spring.

    elastic potential energy = 0.5 × spring constant × (extension)²

    Assuming the spring's limit of proportionality has not been reached, calculate the spring constant of the spring.

    ....

    ....

    ....

    Spring constant = ... N/m
    [3]

Test 42: Physics 1 Mixed Topics

There are **12 questions** in this test. Give yourself **10 minutes** to answer them all.

1. When a person jumps onto a trampoline, energy is transferred from the gravitational potential energy store of the person to the trampoline's elastic potential energy store...

   A ... electrically.

   B ... mechanically.

   C ... by heating.

   [1]

2. A current of 0.2 A flows through a resistor for 4 s. How much charge has passed through the resistor?

   A 0.05 C

   B 0.8 C

   C 3.2 C

   [1]

3. True or False? "A live wire can still be dangerous even when a switch in the mains circuit is open."

   A True

   B False

   [1]

4. True or False? "The higher the temperature of a gas, the slower its particles will move."

   A True

   B False

   [1]

5. The radius of an atom is approximately...

   A ... 1×10^{-12} m.

   B ... 1×10^{10} m.

   C ... 1×10^{-10} m.

   [1]

6. Which of the following correctly describes the energy source used in geothermal power?

   A Energy released by burning plant products.

   B Energy released by hot rocks in the ground.

   [1]

7. True or False? "Some energy is always wasted when an electrical device is used."

   A True

   B False

   [1]

8. A 3 A current flows through two resistors, X and Y. Resistor X's resistance is 10 Ω. Resistor Y's resistance is 5 Ω. Which resistor has the higher potential difference across it?

   A Resistor X

   B Resistor Y

   [1]

Physics Paper 1: Mixed Topics

9. An *I-V* graph for a circuit component is shown on the right. Identify the component.

   Component: ....
   [1]

10. A student has a source of radiation that emits one of the three types of ionising nuclear radiation. He wants to identify the type of radiation that it emits.

    What type of radiation would it be if it was stopped by a sheet of paper?

    ....

    What type of radiation would it be if it was stopped by a sheet of aluminium, but not paper?

    ....
    [2]

11. Silver has a specific latent heat of fusion of 111 000 J/kg. The equation below links the thermal energy for a change of state with the mass of a material and its specific latent heat.

    thermal energy for a change of state = mass × specific latent heat

    Calculate the minimum amount of energy needed to melt 0.25 kg of silver.

    ....

    ....

    Energy = ... J
    [2]

12. 560 J is supplied to an electric pencil sharpener. The pencil sharpener transfers 420 J of this energy usefully. The equation below give the efficiency of a device.

    efficiency = useful output energy transfer ÷ total input energy transfer

    Calculate the efficiency of the pencil sharpener.

    ....

    ....

    Efficiency = ...
    [2]

Physics Paper 2

Test 43: Forces

There are **11 questions** in this test. Give yourself **10 minutes** to answer them all.

1. True or False? "The greater the speed of a car, the greater its stopping distance."

   A   True
   B   False
   [1]

2. A teapot is at rest on a table. The teapot exerts a force of 10 N on the table. What force does the table exert on the teapot?

   A   0 N
   B   –10 N
   C   –20 N
   [1]

3. Which equation correctly links weight, W, mass, m, and gravitational field strength, g?

   A $W = g \div m$
   B $W = m \times g$
   C $W = m \div g$
   [1]

4. What is the gradient of a distance-time graph equal to?

   A   Acceleration
   B   Distance
   C   Speed
   [1]

5. Which of these quantities is not a vector?

   A   Speed
   B   Force
   C   Displacement
   [1]

6. True or False? "A typical person's reaction time is between 2 and 3 seconds."

   A   True
   B   False
   [1]

7. True or False? "If an object is moving, there must be a non-zero resultant force acting on it."

   A   True
   B   False
   [1]

8. True or False? "For an elastic object, extension is directly proportional to the force applied."

   A   True
   B   False
   [1]

Physics Paper 2: Forces

9. A skydiver falling through the air will eventually stop accelerating and travel at a constant speed.

   What is the name given to this speed?

   ....

   What is the resultant force on the skydiver when they are travelling at a constant speed?

   ....
   [2]

10. A student runs at a speed of 3.5 m/s for 26 seconds.

    What equation links distance travelled, speed and time?

    ....

    Calculate the distance the student runs during this time.

    ....

    ....

    Distance = ... m
    [3]

11. The graph on the right shows the velocity of an object over time.

    Describe the acceleration of the object between times C and E.

    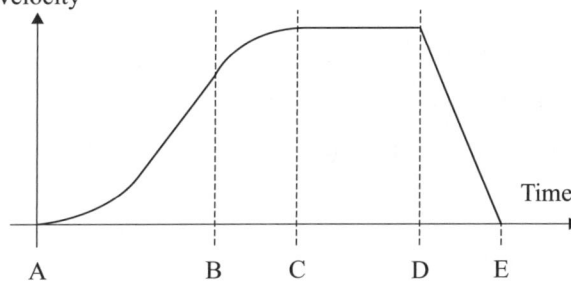

    ....

    ....

    ....

    ....
    [2]

Test 44: Forces

There are **12 questions** in this test. Give yourself **10 minutes** to answer them all.

1. True or False? "When an object does work against frictional forces, it can cause the object to heat up."
   A True
   B False
   [1]

2. The acceleration of an object is equal to...
   A ... the change in its velocity over time.
   B ... the change in its height over time.
   [1]

3. Which of these is a typical running speed for a person?
   A 1 m/s
   B 3 m/s
   C 12 m/s
   [1]

4. A resultant force of 4 N acts on a 2 kg mass. What is the acceleration of the mass?
   A 0.5 m/s^2
   B 2 m/s^2
   C 8 m/s^2
   [1]

5. Which of these does not affect the braking distance of a car?
   A The car's speed
   B The condition of the car's tyres
   C The driver's reaction time
   [1]

6. Stopping distance is equal to...
   A ... thinking distance + braking distance.
   B ... thinking distance − braking distance.
   C ... thinking distance × braking distance.
   [1]

7. What is the name of the point from which the weight of an object can be considered to act?
   A The centre of mass
   B The centre of weight
   [1]

8. According to Newton's Third Law, when two objects interact, the forces they exert on each other are...
   A ... equal and in the same direction.
   B ... equal and in opposite directions.
   [1]

Physics Paper 2: Forces

9. What is the difference between speed and velocity?

....

....
[1]

10. Name two things that can affect a person's reaction time.

1. ....

2. ....
[2]

11. A spring is extended elastically by 0.20 m. It has a spring constant of 30 N/m.
It has not been stretched beyond its limit of proportionality.
Calculate the work done in stretching the spring.

elastic potential energy = 0.5 × spring constant × (extension)^2

....

....

Work done = ... J
[2]

12. This distance-time graph shows the motion of a car.

Calculate the speed of the car during the first 30 seconds of its journey.

....

....

Speed = ... m/s
[2]

Test 45: Forces

There are **11 questions** in this test. Give yourself **10 minutes** to answer them all.

1. True or False? "Mass is the force acting on an object due to gravity."

   A   True

   B   False

   [1]

2. If the resultant force acting on a moving object is zero, the object will...

   A   ... slow down and eventually stop.

   B   ... keep moving at a steady speed.

   [1]

3. A car accelerates from 0 m/s to 10 m/s in 2 s. What is the average acceleration of the car?

   A   2 m/s^2

   B   5 m/s^2

   C   10 m/s^2

   [1]

4. What is the typical speed of sound in air?

   A   330 m/s

   B 3×10^8 m/s

   C   3.3 m/s

   [1]

5. What is a contact force?

   A   A force which can only act when two objects are physically touching.

   B   A force which can act when two objects are physically separated.

   [1]

6. A car is travelling at 30 mph. Which of the following is a sensible estimate for the stopping distance of the car?

   A   5 m

   B   15 m

   C   25 m

   [1]

7. Which of these is true?

   A   When an object falls, work is done against gravity.

   B   When an object is lifted, work is done against gravity.

   [1]

8. A 1 kg ball and a 2 kg ball each have a 2 N force applied to them. Which ball will have the greatest acceleration?

   A   The 1 kg ball

   B   The 2 kg ball

   [1]

Physics Paper 2: Forces

9. A spring is stretched elastically. The limit of proportionality is not exceeded.

What is the minimum number of forces needed to stretch the spring?

....

Write down the equation that links force, extension and the spring constant.

....
[2]

10. The graph on the right shows the motion of a cyclist. Describe the cyclist's motion during the 20 s shown.

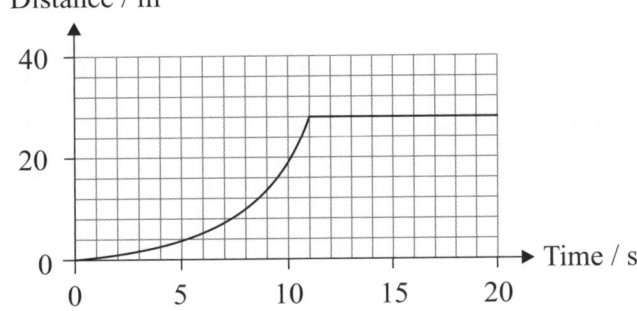

....

....

....
[2]

11. A builder does 84 J of work lifting some bricks from the ground to a height of 1.2 m.

Calculate the force exerted by the builder to lift the bricks.

work done = force × distance

....

....

Force = ... N
[3]

15

Test 46: Waves

There are **12 questions** in this test. Give yourself **10 minutes** to answer them all.

1. True or False? "Our eyes can detect all types of electromagnetic waves."
   A   True
   B   False
   [1]

2. The different types of electromagnetic waves...
   A   ... all have the same wavelength.
   B   ... all have the same frequency.
   C   ... form a continuous spectrum.
   [1]

3. What units are used for wave speed?
   A   Metres per second, m/s
   B   Hertz, Hz
   [1]

4. X-rays can kill body cells because they are...
   A   ... longitudinal waves.
   B   ... ionising.
   [1]

5. True or False? "Changes in atoms can cause electromagnetic waves to be absorbed or emitted."
   A   True
   B   False
   [1]

6. What is the 'normal' on a ray diagram?
   A   A line drawn at 45° to a surface at the point where a wave hits the boundary
   B   A line drawn at 90° to a surface at the point where a wave hits the boundary
   [1]

7. True or False? "Radio waves are used for television broadcasts."
   A   True
   B   False
   [1]

8. Which of the following correctly describes 'radiation dose'?
   A   It is the total radiation that a person is exposed to.
   B   It is the probability of a person being exposed to radiation during an average day.
   C   It is a measure of the risk of harm to a person from exposure to radiation.
   [1]

Physics Paper 2: Waves

9. Give two uses of infrared radiation.

   1. ....

   2. ....
   [2]

10. What are transverse waves?

    ....

    ....
    [1]

11. A pebble is dropped into a pond and creates water ripples. Explain why a leaf on the surface of the water is not carried across the pond by the ripples.

    ....

    ....
    [1]

12. A student uses the equipment shown in the diagram below to form a wave on a string.

    The student measures the length of half a wavelength using a ruler. Describe how she could use this measurement and information from the signal generator to calculate the speed of the wave on the string.

    ....

    ....

    ....

    ....
    [3]

Test 47: Waves

There are **12 questions** in this test. Give yourself **10 minutes** to answer them all.

1. Which of these is a use of gamma radiation?

   A Cooking food

   B Communications

   C Medical imaging

   [1]

2. Refraction is the process in which light...

   A ... bounces back as it hits a new medium.

   B ... changes direction as it enters a new medium.

   C ... transfers all its energy to the medium as it enters that new medium.

   [1]

3. True or False? "Waves transfer matter."

   A True

   B False

   [1]

4. For a longitudinal wave, the vibrations are...

   A ... parallel to the direction of energy transfer.

   B ... perpendicular to the direction of energy transfer.

   [1]

5. True or False? "Waves are only refracted if they're travelling along the normal to the boundary they are crossing."

   A True

   B False

   [1]

6. Which of the following electromagnetic waves has the lowest frequency?

   A Ultraviolet

   B Visible light

   C Infrared

   [1]

7. Which of these is an example of a longitudinal wave?

   A Ripples on the surface of water

   B Sound waves

   C X-rays

   [1]

8. Which of the following statements about electromagnetic (EM) waves is correct?

   A All EM waves travel through a vacuum at the same speed.

   B The higher the frequency of an EM wave, the faster it travels through a vacuum.

   [1]

Physics Paper 2: Waves

9. Give one negative effect of ultraviolet radiation on the body.

   ....
   [1]

10. The following equation links the wave speed, frequency and wavelength of a wave.

    wave speed = frequency × wavelength

    Calculate the speed of a wave with a frequency of 6.0×10^7 Hz and a wavelength of 1.4 m.

    ....

    ....

    Wave speed = ... m/s
    [2]

11. A light ray enters the block to the right at an angle to the normal. The block has a higher optical density than air. Sketch a light ray on the ray diagram to the right to show how the light ray may refract when it enters the block from air.

    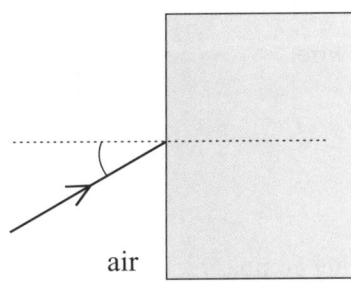

    [1]

12. Calculate the frequency of the wave shown in the graph on the right.

    $$\text{period} = \frac{1}{\text{frequency}}$$

    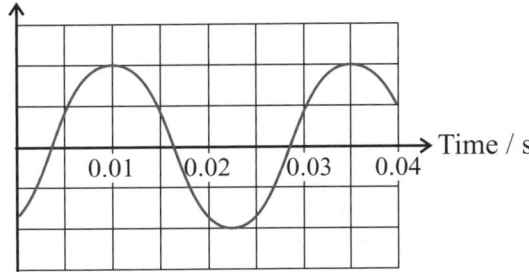

    ....

    ....

    ....

    Frequency = ... Hz
    [3]

Test 48: Magnetism and Electromagnetism

There are **12 questions** in this test. Give yourself **10 minutes** to answer them all.

1. True or False? "The magnetic field of a bar magnet is strongest at the poles."
   - A True
   - B False

   [1]

2. The force between the north poles of two bar magnets is...
   - A ...attractive.
   - B ...repulsive.

   [1]

3. The magnetic field produced when current flows through a wire...
   - A ... goes round the wire in circles centred on the wire.
   - B ... is parallel to the wire.

   [1]

4. Which of the following is a magnetic material?
   - A Copper
   - B Silver
   - C Nickel

   [1]

5. True or False? "A plotting compass tells you the strength of a magnetic field."
   - A True
   - B False

   [1]

6. True or False? "A magnetic material is always repelled by a permanent magnet."
   - A True
   - B False

   [1]

7. A lump of unmagnetised iron becomes an induced magnet when placed next to a bar magnet. When the bar magnet is removed, the magnetic field strength of the iron...
   - A ... decreases.
   - B ... increases.
   - C ... stays the same.

   [1]

8. An iron core can be placed in the middle of a solenoid to...
   - A ... remove the magnetic field of the solenoid.
   - B ... increase the magnetic field strength of the solenoid.

   [1]

Physics Paper 2: Magnetism and Electromagnetism

9. Define what is meant by a magnetic field.

   ....

   ....
   [1]

10. A bar magnet is shown below. Draw the magnetic field pattern of the bar magnet on the diagram. Include arrows on your field lines to show the direction of the field.

    | N   S |

    [2]

11. State two ways in which the magnetic field strength of a current-carrying wire can be increased.

    1. ....

    ....

    2. ....

    ....
    [2]

12. State the approximate direction in which a compass will point if it is not near to any magnetised materials. Explain why the compass points in this direction.

    ....

    ....

    ....
    [2]

Test 49: Physics 2 Mixed Topics

There are **12 questions** in this test. Give yourself **10 minutes** to answer them all.

1. The direction of the arrow on a magnetic field line at a point is given by the direction of the force that would act on...

   A ... a north pole placed at that point.

   B ... a south pole placed at that point.

   [1]

2. The magnetic field inside a solenoid is...

   A ... weak and uniform.

   B ... strong and uniform.

   C ... strong and irregular.

   [1]

3. Which of these is a typical walking speed?

   A 1.5 m/s

   B 4.5 m/s

   [1]

4. Which of the equations below correctly links work done, W, by a force, F, to the distance moved along the line of action of the force, s?

   A $W = F \div s$

   B $W = s \div F$

   C $W = F \times s$

   [1]

5. X-rays are...

   A ... electromagnetic waves.

   B ... sound waves.

   C ... radio waves.

   [1]

6. For a car to travel at a constant speed, the driving force of the car engine must...

   A ... be less than the frictional forces.

   B ... balance the frictional forces.

   C ... be greater than the frictional forces.

   [1]

7. Which of the following is a correct statement of a displacement?

   A 10 m/s north

   B 10 m

   C 10 m north

   [1]

8. The amplitude of a wave is...

   A ... the distance between the same point on two adjacent waves.

   B ... the maximum displacement of a point on a wave from its undisturbed position.

   [1]

Physics Paper 2: Mixed Topics

9. State one useful application of microwaves.

....
[1]

10. What will happen to a piece of cobalt if it is placed in a magnetic field?

....
[1]

11. A velocity-time graph for a racing car is shown on the right.

Calculate the acceleration of the car during the first 10 s of its journey.

....

....

Acceleration = ... m/s^2
[2]

12. A student sets up water waves with a frequency of 4.0 Hz in a ripple tank. He measures the distance shown in the diagram to be 8.4 cm.

State the equation linking wave speed, frequency and wavelength.

....

Calculate the speed of the waves.

....

....

....

Wave speed = ... m/s
[3]

Test 50: Physics 2 Mixed Topics

There are **12 questions** in this test. Give yourself **10 minutes** to answer them all.

1. True or False? "When a magnetic material is placed in a magnetic field, it always feels a force of attraction."

   A   True

   B   False

   [1]

2. Which of these is a contact force?

   A   Gravitational force

   B   Electrostatic force

   C   Air resistance

   [1]

3. Which electromagnetic wave can make skin age prematurely?

   A   Visible light

   B   Ultraviolet

   [1]

4. What is the frequency of a wave?

   A   The distance travelled by the wave each second.

   B   The number of complete waves passing a point per second.

   [1]

5. Which of these is a typical value for a person's reaction time?

   A   0.04 s

   B   0.4 s

   C   4 s

   [1]

6. Which of these is a vector quantity?

   A   Speed

   B   Distance

   C   Force

   [1]

7. When two unlike magnetic poles are brought together, they...

   A   ... attract each other.

   B   ... repel each other.

   [1]

8. Two toy cars with the same mass are pushed with different forces. The car pushed with a greater force has...

   A   ... a greater acceleration than the other car.

   B   ... a lower acceleration than the other car.

   C   ... the same acceleration as the other car.

   [1]

9. A student suspends a spring from a clamp and hangs different masses from it. She plots the force exerted by each mass against the extension of the spring that it produces on the graph on the right. What is the gradient of this graph equal to?

　..
　[1]

10. How much force would be needed to accelerate a 24 kg object by 3.0 m/s²?

$$\text{force} = \text{mass} \times \text{acceleration}$$

....

....

Force = ... N
[2]

11. A skydiver has a weight of 750 N. The drag acting upwards on the skydiver is 600 N. What is the resultant vertical force acting on the skydiver?

....

....

Force = ... N   Direction = ...
[2]

12. The diagram on the right shows a metal cube with one face that has been painted black and one face that has been painted white. The cube is filled with hot water and each face is measured to be the same temperature. Describe how you could determine which face is the better emitter of infrared radiation.

....

....

....

....
[2]

Answers

Biology Paper 1

Test 1: Cell Biology
Pages 2–3
1. A *[1 mark]*
2. A *[1 mark]*
3. B *[1 mark]*
4. A *[1 mark]*
5. C *[1 mark]*
6. B *[1 mark]*
7. A *[1 mark]*
8. B *[1 mark]*
9. Any one from: e.g. paralysis / diabetes *[1 mark]*.
10. E.g. a nerve cell is long / has branched connections at its ends *[1 mark]*.
11. Because the concentration of mineral ions in the soil is usually lower than in the root hair cells *[1 mark]*. Active transport *[1 mark]*
12.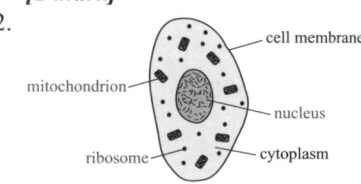
    [1 mark for each correct label] Mitochondria are where most of the reactions for aerobic respiration take place *[1 mark]*

Test 2: Organisation
Pages 4–5
1. B *[1 mark]*
2. A *[1 mark]*
3. A *[1 mark]*
4. C *[1 mark]*
5. B *[1 mark]*
6. B *[1 mark]*
7. A *[1 mark]*
8. A *[1 mark]*
9. E.g. drinking too much alcohol *[1 mark]*.
10. It increases it *[1 mark]*.
11. Protease enzymes catalyse the breakdown of proteins into amino acids *[1 mark]*.
12. The enzyme's unique shape changes / the enzyme denatures *[1 mark]*. The enzyme won't work any more *[1 mark]*.
13. Any two from: e.g. red blood cells, white blood cells, platelets *[2 marks]*

Test 3: Organisation
Pages 6–7
1. B *[1 mark]*
2. B *[1 mark]*
3. A *[1 mark]*
4. B *[1 mark]*
5. B *[1 mark]*
6. B *[1 mark]*
7. A *[1 mark]*
8. A *[1 mark]*
9. In the right atrium *[1 mark]*.
10. Any two from: e.g. stress / diet / life situation (e.g. lack of money) *[2 marks]*.
11. Any two from: e.g. arteries carry blood away from the heart, whilst veins carry blood to the heart. / Arteries have thick walls, whilst veins have thin walls. / Veins contain valves, but arteries don't. *[2 marks]*
12. They decrease it *[1 mark]*. Coronary heart disease *[1 mark]*

Test 4: Infection and Response
Pages 8–9
1. A *[1 mark]*
2. A *[1 mark]*
3. C *[1 mark]*
4. B *[1 mark]*
5. A *[1 mark]*
6. C *[1 mark]*
7. B *[1 mark]*
8. B *[1 mark]*
9. foxglove *[1 mark]*
10. By using fungicides / destroying infected leaves *[1 mark]*.
11. Because it means the plant can't photosynthesise as much *[1 mark]*.
12. The nose contains hairs / mucus *[1 mark]*, which trap particles that could contain pathogens *[1 mark]*.
13. E.g. by stopping mosquitoes from breeding *[1 mark]*. By using mosquito nets to stop people being bitten *[1 mark]*.

Test 5: Infection and Response
Pages 10–11
1. B *[1 mark]*
2. B *[1 mark]*
3. B *[1 mark]*
4. C *[1 mark]*
5. A *[1 mark]*
6. B *[1 mark]*
7. B *[1 mark]*
8. A *[1 mark]*
9. A drug that kills bacteria *[1 mark]*.
10. Measles is spread by droplets from an infected person's sneeze or cough *[1 mark]*.
11. Inside cells *[1 mark]*. The cell will burst, releasing all the viruses, and this cell damage is what makes you feel ill *[1 mark]*.
12. The dead or inactive pathogens that the vaccine contains carry antigens *[1 mark]*. White blood cells produce antibodies in response to these antigens *[1 mark]*. If the same type of pathogens appear after that, the white blood cells can quickly mass-produce the same antibodies to kill the pathogens *[1 mark]*.

Test 6: Bioenergetics
Pages 12–13
1. C *[1 mark]*
2. A *[1 mark]*
3. A *[1 mark]*
4. C *[1 mark]*
5. A *[1 mark]*
6. A *[1 mark]*
7. A *[1 mark]*
8. A *[1 mark]*
9. Because the body can't supply oxygen quickly enough to sustain aerobic respiration *[1 mark]*.
10. Cellulose *[1 mark]*. The cell wall is made using this material *[1 mark]*.
11.
$$\text{carbon dioxide} + \text{water} \xrightarrow{\text{light}} \text{glucose} + \text{oxygen}$$

[2 marks for whole equation completed correctly, or 1 mark for one or two gaps filled correctly.]

Answers

12. Any two from: e.g. in chemical reactions to build up larger molecules from smaller ones. / To allow the muscles to contract/ for movement. / To keep body temperature steady in colder surroundings/to keep warm. *[2 marks]*

Test 7: Bioenergetics
Pages 14–15
1. B *[1 mark]* 2. B *[1 mark]*
3. A *[1 mark]* 4. B *[1 mark]*
5. B *[1 mark]* 6. A *[1 mark]*
7. B *[1 mark]* 8. A *[1 mark]*
9. Metabolism is the sum of all the reactions that happen in a cell or the body *[1 mark]*.
10. It will slow down *[1 mark]*. Because there will be less light present to transfer the energy needed for photosynthesis *[1 mark]*.
11. Muscle fatigue is where the muscles tire and can no longer contract efficiently *[1 mark]*. It can occur during long periods of exercise *[1 mark]*.
12. starch *[1 mark]*, cellulose *[1 mark]*

Test 8: Biology 1 Mixed Topics
Pages 16–17
1. B *[1 mark]* 2. B *[1 mark]*
3. A *[1 mark]* 4. A *[1 mark]*
5. B *[1 mark]* 6. B *[1 mark]*
7. B *[1 mark]* 8. A *[1 mark]*
9. $$\text{magnification} = \frac{\text{size of image}}{\text{size of real object}}$$
   [1 mark]
10. Any two from: It has a thin membrane. / It has a large surface area. / It has lots of blood vessels. / It could be ventilated. *[2 marks]*
11. E.g. temperature *[1 mark]*. By using a water bath / an electric heater. *[1 mark]*

12. It increases the rate of diffusion *[1 mark]*, because more particles can pass across the exchange surface at once *[1 mark]*.

Test 9: Biology 1 Mixed Topics
Pages 18–19
1. C *[1 mark]* 2. B *[1 mark]*
3. A *[1 mark]* 4. B *[1 mark]*
5. A *[1 mark]* 6. A *[1 mark]*
7. B *[1 mark]* 8. A *[1 mark]*
9. Any one from: e.g. skin / nose / stomach / trachea and bronchi *[1 mark]*.
10. Pulmonary vein *[1 mark]* Aorta *[1 mark]*
11. Any two from: e.g. cardiovascular disease / lung disease / lung cancer *[2 marks]*
12. Blood flow through the coronary arteries is reduced *[1 mark]*, resulting in a lack of oxygen for the heart muscle *[1 mark]*.

Biology Paper 2

Test 10: Homeostasis and Response
Pages 20–21
1. A *[1 mark]* 2. B *[1 mark]*
3. A *[1 mark]* 4. C *[1 mark]*
5. B *[1 mark]* 6. A *[1 mark]*
7. B *[1 mark]* 8. B *[1 mark]*
9. A receptor detects a stimulus *[1 mark]*.
10. E.g. because it means that a person's blood sugar level can rise to a level that can kill them *[1 mark]*.
11.

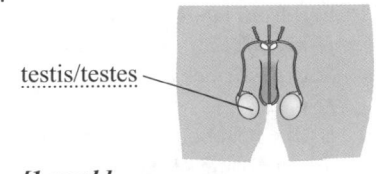

[1 mark]
Testosterone *[1 mark]*

12. Homeostasis is the regulation of conditions inside the body *[1 mark]* to maintain a stable internal environment *[1 mark]* in response to changes in internal and external conditions *[1 mark]*.

Test 11: Homeostasis and Response
Pages 22–23
1. B *[1 mark]* 2. B *[1 mark]*
3. B *[1 mark]* 4. B *[1 mark]*
5. A *[1 mark]* 6. C *[1 mark]*
7. B *[1 mark]* 8. A *[1 mark]*
9. It stimulates the release of an egg from the ovary *[1 mark]*.
10. E.g. eating a carbohydrate- controlled diet *[1 mark]*. Regular exercise *[1 mark]*.
11. Any two from: e.g. water content of the blood. / Core body temperature. / Blood sugar level. *[2 marks]*
12. A motor neurone *[1 mark]*. Examples: Muscle (e.g. biceps) / A gland (e.g. adrenal gland) *[1 mark]*.

Test 12: Inheritance, Variation and Evolution
Pages 24–25
1. A *[1 mark]* 2. A *[1 mark]*
3. A *[1 mark]* 4. B *[1 mark]*
5. B *[1 mark]* 6. B *[1 mark]*
7. B *[1 mark]* 8. A *[1 mark]*
9. Differences in characteristics between individuals *[1 mark]*.
10. A gene from one organism is 'cut out' and put into another organism's cells *[1 mark]*. This gives the new organism a new, useful characteristic *[1 mark]*.

Answers

11. Any two from: e.g. the environment changes too quickly. / A new predator. / A new disease. / Competition with another, more successful species for resources. / A catastrophic event, e.g. a volcanic eruption. *[2 marks]*
12. Yes *[1 mark]*. Because they have a common ancestor *[1 mark]*.

Test 13: Inheritance, Variation and Evolution
Pages 26–27

1. A *[1 mark]* 2. A *[1 mark]*
3. B *[1 mark]* 4. A *[1 mark]*
5. B *[1 mark]* 6. A *[1 mark]*
7. B *[1 mark]* 8. B *[1 mark]*
9. A double helix *[1 mark]*
10. Any one from: e.g. it has been shown that characteristics/traits are passed on to offspring in genes. / The evidence in the fossil record. / The evolution of antibiotic resistance in bacteria. *[1 mark]*
11.

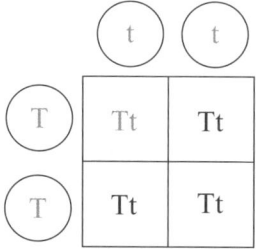

[2 marks for all three genotypes correct, or 1 mark for two correct]

12. During sexual reproduction two gametes fuse together, producing a new cell *[1 mark]*. This cell contains a mixture of chromosomes — some from the mother, and some from the father *[1 mark]*. This means it inherits a combination of features from each parent, producing variation *[1 mark]*.

Test 14: Ecology
Pages 28–29

1. B *[1 mark]* 2. B *[1 mark]*
3. A *[1 mark]* 4. B *[1 mark]*
5. B *[1 mark]* 6. A *[1 mark]*
7. B *[1 mark]* 8. A *[1 mark]*
9. interdependence *[1 mark]*
10. It releases carbon dioxide into the air *[1 mark]*.
11. A feature/characteristic that allows an organism to survive in certain environmental conditions *[1 mark]*.
12. Any two from: e.g. new pathogens arriving. / New predators arriving. / The availability of food. / An increase in the number or type of competitors. *[2 marks]*
13. Any two from: e.g. breeding programmes. / Programmes to regenerate rare habitats. / Programmes to reintroduce field margins and hedgerows to farm land. / Programmes to reduce deforestation. / Programmes to reduce carbon dioxide emissions. / Programmes to encourage people to recycle waste. *[2 marks]*

Test 15: Ecology
Pages 30-31

1. A *[1 mark]* 2. B *[1 mark]*
3. A *[1 mark]* 4. B *[1 mark]*
5. C *[1 mark]* 6. B *[1 mark]*
7. A *[1 mark]* 8. B *[1 mark]*
9. A community where all the species and environmental factors are in balance *[1 mark]*.
10. E.g. to provide land for cattle/rice crops/farming *[1 mark]*. To grow crops for biofuels *[1 mark]*.
11. E.g. from landfill waste *[1 mark]*. From toxic chemicals (e.g. pesticides and herbicides) *[1 mark]*.
12. By the peat being broken down/decomposing *[1 mark]*.
    By the peat being burned *[1 mark]*.

Test 16: Biology 2 Mixed Topics
Pages 32–33

1. B *[1 mark]* 2. A *[1 mark]*
3. C *[1 mark]* 4. B *[1 mark]*
5. A *[1 mark]* 6. A *[1 mark]*
7. B *[1 mark]* 8. B *[1 mark]*
9. It produces a response to a nervous impulse *[1 mark]*.
10. E.g. (human) insulin *[1 mark]*
11. It's when no individuals of the species remain *[1 mark]*.
12. Any two from: Eukaryota / Archaea / Bacteria *[2 marks]*
13. E.g. people aren't immune to the new strain *[1 mark]*. There is no effective treatment *[1 mark]*.

Test 17: Biology 2 Mixed Topics
Pages 34–35

1. B *[1 mark]* 2. B *[1 mark]*
3. B *[1 mark]* 4. A *[1 mark]*
5. B *[1 mark]* 6. B *[1 mark]*
7. A *[1 mark]* 8. A *[1 mark]*
9. Alex is male *[1 mark]*. (Females have two X chromosomes, males have an X and a Y chromosome.)
10. Any two from: e.g. oral contraceptive pill / skin patch / implant / injection *[2 marks]*.
11. Where a person becomes resistant to their own insulin *[1 mark]*. E.g. obesity *[1 mark]*
12. Inbreeding is when closely related individuals are bred together *[1 mark]*. Because it increases the chance that an individual will inherit harmful genetic defects *[1 mark]*.

Answers

Chemistry Paper 1

Test 18: Atomic Structure and the Periodic Table
Pages 36–37
1. A *[1 mark]*
2. C *[1 mark]*
3. B *[1 mark]*
4. A *[1 mark]*
5. B *[1 mark]*
6. B *[1 mark]*
7. B *[1 mark]*
8. C *[1 mark]*
9. They have the same number of outer electrons/electrons in their outer shell *[1 mark]*.
10. The reactivity increases *[1 mark]*.
11. Proton — +1
    Neutron — no charge
    Electron — –1
    [1 mark for two correct, 2 marks for all three correct answers]
12. It has too many electrons in the first shell / the first shell should only hold two electrons *[1 mark]*.
13. They have the same number of protons/are the same element *[1 mark]* but have a different number of neutrons *[1 mark]*.

Test 19: Bonding, Structure and Properties
Pages 38–39
1. A *[1 mark]*
2. A *[1 mark]*
3. B *[1 mark]*
4. C *[1 mark]*
5. C *[1 mark]*
6. C *[1 mark]*
7. A *[1 mark]*
8. A *[1 mark]*
9. Covalent bonding *[1 mark]*
10. E.g. it is very hard. / It has a very high melting point. / It doesn't conduct electricity. *[1 mark]*
11. Sodium/Na^+ ions and chloride/Cl^- ions *[1 mark]*
    Electrostatic forces *[1 mark]*
12. It takes a lot of energy to break the intermolecular forces between the polymer molecules *[1 mark]*.
13. A *[1 mark]*
    The delocalised electrons can carry electrical charge *[1 mark]*.

Test 20: Bonding, Structure and Properties
Pages 40–41
1. A *[1 mark]*
2. B *[1 mark]*
3. A *[1 mark]*
4. C *[1 mark]*
5. A *[1 mark]*
6. B *[1 mark]*
7. B *[1 mark]*
8. A *[1 mark]*
9. Outer electrons are transferred from the metal atom to the non-metal atom *[1 mark]*.
10. Fullerenes *[1 mark]*
    E.g. in electronics / to strengthen materials / to deliver drugs / as lubricants / as catalysts *[1 mark]*.
11. The atoms are arranged in layers *[1 mark]* which can slide over each other *[1 mark]*.
12. A polymer *[1 mark]*
13. Ethanol (it boils at 78°C) *[1 mark]*

Test 21: Quantitative Chemistry
Pages 42–43
1. B *[1 mark]*
2. B *[1 mark]*
3. C *[1 mark]*
4. A *[1 mark]*
5. A *[1 mark]*
6. B *[1 mark]*
7. B *[1 mark]*
8. A *[1 mark]*
9. A_r of Li = 7, A_r of O = 16 *[1 mark]*
   M_r of Li_2O = 7 + 7 + 16 = 30 *[1 mark]*
10. 13 – 9 = 4 cm³ *[1 mark]*.
11. $2Al_2O_{3(l)} \rightarrow 4Al_{(l)} + 3O_{2(g)}$
    [1 mark for correct left hand side, 1 mark for correct right hand side]
12. concentration = mass ÷ volume
    Rearrange to:
    mass = conc. × volume *[1 mark]*
    = 0.50 × 0.50 = 0.25 g *[1 mark]*

Test 22: Chemical Changes
Pages 44–45
1. C *[1 mark]*
2. A *[1 mark]*
3. A *[1 mark]*
4. B *[1 mark]*
5. A *[1 mark]*
6. A *[1 mark]*
7. B *[1 mark]*
8. C *[1 mark]*
9. Hydrogen *[1 mark]* and chlorine *[1 mark]*
10. Magnesium reacts more vigorously than iron *[1 mark]*, because magnesium is higher than iron in the reactivity series / is more reactive than iron *[1 mark]*.
11. The ions are not free to move *[1 mark]*.
12. Aluminium / any metal above carbon in the reactivity series *[1 mark]*.
    It's too reactive to be extracted by reduction with carbon. / It's above carbon in the reactivity series. *[1 mark]*.

Test 23: Energy Changes
Pages 46–47
1. A *[1 mark]*
2. B *[1 mark]*
3. B *[1 mark]*
4. B *[1 mark]*
5. B *[1 mark]*
6. B *[1 mark]*
7. B *[1 mark]*
8. B *[1 mark]*
9. Not all particles collide with enough energy to react *[1 mark]*.
10. Exothermic reactions transfer energy to the surroundings. Therefore the temperature of the surroundings, including the hands, increases *[1 mark]*.
11. E.g. combustion / neutralisation / many oxidation reactions *[1 mark]*
12. An exothermic reaction *[1 mark]*. The products are at a lower energy than the reactants *[1 mark]*.
    Overall energy change = B *[1 mark]*
    Activation energy = A *[1 mark]*

Test 24: Chemistry 1 Mixed Topics
Pages 48–49
1. B *[1 mark]*
2. A *[1 mark]*
3. B *[1 mark]*
4. A *[1 mark]*
5. B *[1 mark]*
6. A *[1 mark]*
7. A *[1 mark]*
8. B *[1 mark]*
9. Giant covalent structure *[1 mark]*
10. Metal A is more reactive than metal B *[1 mark]*.

Answers

11. A metal salt *[1 mark]* and hydrogen *[1 mark]*
12. The mass of the products in a reaction is equal to the mass of the reactants *[1 mark]*.
    CO_2 was released as a gas during the reaction *[1 mark]*. This gas was lost from the open beaker and so its mass was not measured *[1 mark]*.

Test 25: Chemistry 1 Mixed Topics
Pages 50–51

1. B *[1 mark]*
2. C *[1 mark]*
3. A *[1 mark]*
4. B *[1 mark]*
5. A *[1 mark]*
6. A *[1 mark]*
7. B *[1 mark]*
8. B *[1 mark]*
9. Chlorine is more reactive than bromine so displaces it from the salt *[1 mark]*.
   No reaction will occur between bromine vapour and potassium chloride solution *[1 mark]*.
10. Negative electrode/cathode *[1 mark]*
11. It has four electrons in its outer shell *[1 mark]*, so it must be in group 4 *[1 mark]*.
12. proton: 1
    neutron: 1
    electron: very small *[1 mark for all three answers]*
13. The pH of a substance tells you how acidic or alkaline it is *[1 mark]*.

Chemistry Paper 2

Test 26: Rate and Extent of Chemical Change
Pages 52–53

1. B *[1 mark]*
2. A *[1 mark]*
3. B *[1 mark]*
4. A *[1 mark]*
5. B *[1 mark]*
6. B *[1 mark]*
7. A *[1 mark]*
8. C *[1 mark]*
9. Rate of reaction = amount of product formed ÷ time taken *[1 mark]*
   Rate of reaction = 30 cm³ ÷ 12 s
   = 2.5 cm³/s
   [1 mark for correct answer, 1 mark for correct units]
10. Experiment 2 *[1 mark]*
    The temperature/concentration of reactants/pressure (with gases) could have been increased. / A catalyst could have been used / Solid reactants may have been crushed into smaller parts *[1 mark]*.
11. The surface area of the solid is increased *[1 mark]*, meaning there are more frequent collisions between reactants *[1 mark]*.

Test 27: Rate and Extent of Chemical Change
Pages 54–55

1. B *[1 mark]*
2. B *[1 mark]*
3. A *[1 mark]*
4. B *[1 mark]*
5. B *[1 mark]*
6. B *[1 mark]*
7. B *[1 mark]*
8. A *[1 mark]*
9. The forward and reverse reactions are occurring at exactly the same rate *[1 mark]*.
10. The volume of O_2 produced will stay the same *[1 mark]*. The presence of a catalyst doesn't affect the amount of O_2 produced. / The total volume of O_2 produced is only affected by the initial amount of H_2O_2 *[1 mark]*.
11. Increasing the pressure of reacting gases reduces the space the reactant particles are in / increases the number of reactant particles in a given volume *[1 mark]* so will increase the frequency of collisions *[1 mark]*.

12. Mass of gas given off = 150 − 147 = 3 g
    Rate of reaction = Amount of product formed ÷ time = 3 ÷ 40 *[1 mark]* = 0.075 g/s *[1 mark]*

Test 28: Organic Chemistry
Pages 56–57

1. B *[1 mark]*
2. B *[1 mark]*
3. A *[1 mark]*
4. A *[1 mark]*
5. B *[1 mark]*
6. A *[1 mark]*
7. C *[1 mark]*
8. B *[1 mark]*
9.
   $$H-\underset{\underset{H}{|}}{\overset{\overset{H}{|}}{C}}-\underset{\underset{H}{|}}{\overset{\overset{H}{|}}{C}}-H$$
   [1 mark]
   Ethane *[1 mark]*
10. carbon dioxide *[1 mark]*
11. Decane will have a higher boiling point *[1 mark]* because it has a longer hydrocarbon chain *[1 mark]*.
12. Bromine water *[1 mark]*.
    The bromine water would turn colourless *[1 mark]*.

Test 29: Chemical Analysis
Pages 58–59

1. C *[1 mark]*
2. A *[1 mark]*
3. B *[1 mark]*
4. A *[1 mark]*
5. A *[1 mark]*
6. B *[1 mark]*
7. A *[1 mark]*
8. B *[1 mark]*
9. Put damp litmus paper into the gas. Chlorine will turn the litmus paper white / bleach it *[1 mark]*.
10. The water is impure *[1 mark]*.
11. R_f = distance travelled by substance ÷ distance travelled by solvent *[1 mark]*.
    R_f = 3.2 ÷ 5.0 = 0.64 *[1 mark]*
12. Mobile phase and stationary phase *[1 mark]*.
    A pure substance will leave a single spot on the chromatography paper in all solvents *[1 mark]*. An impure substance can leave multiple spots *[1 mark]*.

Answers

Test 30: Chemistry of the Atmosphere
Pages 60–61
1. C *[1 mark]*
2. A *[1 mark]*
3. A *[1 mark]*
4. B *[1 mark]*
5. B *[1 mark]*
6. A *[1 mark]*
7. C *[1 mark]*
8. B *[1 mark]*
9. Oxygen *[1 mark]*
   Photosynthesis *[1 mark]*
10. Any one from, e.g. a rise in sea level / increased flooding / increased coastal erosion *[1 mark]*. Any two from, e.g. changes in rainfall patterns / increased frequency/severity of storms / some regions will struggle to produce enough food / distribution of wildlife will change *[1 mark for each]*.
11. Any two from, e.g. deforestation / any activity which involves burning fossil fuels / breakdown of landfill and farm waste *[2 marks]*.

Test 31: Chemistry of the Atmosphere
Pages 62–63
1. A *[1 mark]*
2. C *[1 mark]*
3. A *[1 mark]*
4. B *[1 mark]*
5. A *[1 mark]*
6. A *[1 mark]*
7. A *[1 mark]*
8. B *[1 mark]*
9. Carbon dioxide *[1 mark]*. Any two from, e.g. methane / ammonia / water vapour / nitrogen *[1 mark]*. From volcanic eruptions *[1 mark]*.
10. E.g. tax companies/individuals based on CO_2 emissions / invest in renewable energy resources/ nuclear power / cap emissions made by companies *[1 mark]*. E.g. concern about impact on economic growth / alternative technologies still need development *[1 mark]*.
11. E.g. agriculture/farming *[1 mark]*, creating waste *[1 mark]*.

Test 32: Using Resources
Pages 64–65
1. A *[1 mark]*
2. C *[1 mark]*
3. B *[1 mark]*
4. B *[1 mark]*
5. B *[1 mark]*
6. B *[1 mark]*
7. B *[1 mark]*
8. B *[1 mark]*
9. E.g. landscape damage / habitat destruction / requires energy that comes from burning fossil fuels, which causes air pollution and increased CO_2 levels *[1 mark]*.
10. Any two from, e.g. bubbling chlorine gas through it. / Using ozone. / Using ultraviolet light *[2 marks]*.
11. Extracting and processing the raw materials *[1 mark]*, manufacturing and packaging *[1 mark]*, using the product *[1 mark]*, disposal of the product *[1 mark]*

Test 33: Chemistry 2 Mixed Topics
Pages 66–67
1. B *[1 mark]*
2. B *[1 mark]*
3. B *[1 mark]*
4. A *[1 mark]*
5. B *[1 mark]*
6. B *[1 mark]*
7. B *[1 mark]*
8. B *[1 mark]*
9. The amount of carbon dioxide and other greenhouse gases *[1 mark]* that are released over a product's full life cycle *[1 mark]*.
10. The frequency of collisions increases *[1 mark]*. The collisions are more energetic *[1 mark]*.
11. Their components are mixed together in measured quantities *[1 mark]*.
12. Put a glowing splint into a test tube of the gas, it will relight if oxygen is present *[1 mark]*.
13. E.g. it takes less energy than mining and extracting metals / it is cheaper than mining metals / the finite amount of metal on Earth is conserved / less waste is produced which must be disposed of in comparison to mining and extracting metals *[1 mark]*.

Test 34: Chemistry 2 Mixed Topics
Pages 68–69
1. A *[1 mark]*
2. A *[1 mark]*
3. A *[1 mark]*
4. C *[1 mark]*
5. B *[1 mark]*
6. C *[1 mark]*
7. B *[1 mark]*
8. A *[1 mark]*
9. Line 2 *[1 mark]*. Line 2 has a lower initial rise in energy than line 1, showing a lower activation energy *[1 mark]*.
10. Bubble the gas through limewater, it will turn milky if carbon dioxide is present *[1 mark]*.
11. Sedimentation *[1 mark]*
    Anaerobic digestion *[1 mark]*
12. Any two from: e.g. green plants/ algae absorbed the carbon dioxide during photosynthesis / it dissolved in the ocean / it became locked up in sedimentary rocks/fossil fuels when they formed *[2 marks]*.

Physics Paper 1

Test 35: Energy
Pages 70–71
1. B *[1 mark]*
2. B *[1 mark]*
3. A *[1 mark]*
4. C *[1 mark]*
5. B *[1 mark]*
6. A *[1 mark]*
7. B *[1 mark]*
8. A *[1 mark]*
9. Any two from: e.g. coal / oil / (natural) gas *[2 marks]*
10. E.g. Radioactive waste is produced, which is difficult to dispose of safely. / It's expensive to set up and close down nuclear power stations. / There is a risk of radiation leaks and catastrophes. *[1 mark]*
11. kinetic energy
    = 0.5 × mass × (speed)^2
    or $E_k = \frac{1}{2}mv^2$
    $= \frac{1}{2} \times 160 \times 10^2$ *[1 mark]*
    = 8000 J *[1 mark]*

Answers

12. change in thermal energy = mass × specific heat capacity × temperature change
    = 0.5 × 400 × 15 *[1 mark]*
    = 3000 J *[1 mark]*

Test 36: Energy
Pages 72–73
1. B *[1 mark]*   2. A *[1 mark]*
3. A *[1 mark]*   4. A *[1 mark]*
5. A *[1 mark]*   6. C *[1 mark]*
7. B *[1 mark]*   8. B *[1 mark]*
9. E.g. the Sun / wind / biofuel / hydro-electricity / geothermal / the tides / water waves *[1 mark]*
10. Block B *[1 mark]*, as it has the lowest temperature change for the given amount of energy supplied *[1 mark]*.
11. A hairdryer transfers energy electrically from the mains to the thermal energy store of the hairdryer heater *[1 mark]* and the kinetic energy store of the fan blades *[1 mark]*.
12. Gravitational potential energy = mass × gravitational field strength × height
    = 0.5 × 9.8 × 30 *[1 mark]*
    = 147 J *[1 mark]*

Test 37: Electricity
Pages 74–75
1. C *[1 mark]*   2. A *[1 mark]*
3. A *[1 mark]*   4. C *[1 mark]*
5. A *[1 mark]*   6. B *[1 mark]*
7. A *[1 mark]*   8. A *[1 mark]*
9. charge flow = energy transferred ÷ potential difference
    = 5400 ÷ 1.2 *[1 mark]*
    = 4500 C *[1 mark]*
10. Resistance is directly proportional to the length of the conductor *[1 mark]*.

11. voltage = current × resistance or $V = IR$ *[1 mark]*
    $V = 3.0 \times 10$ *[1 mark]*
    = 30 V *[1 mark]*
12. Fuse *[1 mark]*

Test 38: Electricity
Pages 76–77
1. B *[1 mark]*   2. B *[1 mark]*
3. A *[1 mark]*   4. B *[1 mark]*
5. B *[1 mark]*   6. A *[1 mark]*
7. B *[1 mark]*   8. C *[1 mark]*
9. Transformers *[1 mark]*
10. Frequency = 50 Hz *[1 mark]*
    Potential difference = 230 V *[1 mark]*
11. In a series circuit, the supply potential difference is shared, so:
    $V_3 = V_1 + V_2 = 3 + 2 = 5$ V *[1 mark]*
    Resistances add up, so:
    $R = R_1 + R_2 = 6 + 4 = 10$ Ω *[1 mark]*
12. current = power ÷ potential difference
    = 57.5 ÷ 230 *[1 mark]*
    = 0.25 A *[1 mark]*

Test 39: Particle Model of Matter
Pages 78–79
1. B *[1 mark]*   2. A *[1 mark]*
3. A *[1 mark]*   4. B *[1 mark]*
5. B *[1 mark]*   6. A *[1 mark]*
7. C *[1 mark]*   8. B *[1 mark]*
9. Joules per kilogram / J/kg *[1 mark]*
10. Particles in a solid are held close together in a regular arrangement, whereas particles in a gas are far apart and are free to move *[1 mark]*.
11. solid *[1 mark]*
12. density = mass ÷ volume
    = $0.386 \div (2.00 \times 10^{-5})$ *[1 mark]*
    = 19 300 kg/m^3 *[1 mark]*

13. E.g. measure the object's length, width and height with a ruler, then use them to calculate its volume (using volume = length × width × height) *[1 mark]*. Measure the object's mass using a balance, then plug the object's mass and volume into density = mass ÷ volume to calculate the density *[1 mark]*.

Test 40: Atomic Structure
Pages 80–81
1. B *[1 mark]*   2. B *[1 mark]*
3. A *[1 mark]*   4. A *[1 mark]*
5. B *[1 mark]*   6. C *[1 mark]*
7. B *[1 mark]*   8. B *[1 mark]*
9. An atom is electrically neutral, but an ion is charged. / An atom has the same number of protons and electrons, but an ion doesn't *[1 mark]*.
10. There are initially 14 000 radioactive nuclei, so after one half-life there will be 7000 radioactive nuclei.
    Reading from graph:
    half-life = 56 years *[1 mark]*
    To fall to one quarter of the initial amount, the number of radioactive nuclei must halve and halve again *[1 mark]*. So the time taken is equal to two half lives, or:
    2 × 56 = 112 years *[1 mark]*
11. The electron orbits further from the nucleus *[1 mark]*.
12. Irradiation is when an object is exposed to radiation emitted by a radioactive source *[1 mark]* while contamination is when (unwanted) atoms of a radioactive source get on/inside another object *[1 mark]*.

Answers

Test 41: Physics 1 Mixed Topics
Pages 82–83
1. A *[1 mark]*   2. B *[1 mark]*
3. B *[1 mark]*   4. C *[1 mark]*
5. A *[1 mark]*   6. B *[1 mark]*
7. B *[1 mark]*   8. A *[1 mark]*
9. It increases *[1 mark]*
10. After one half-life, the number of radioactive nuclei in the sample will halve. So the number of nuclei left
 = $(1.2 \times 10^5) \div 2$
 = 6.0×10^4 *[1 mark]*
11. $^{241}_{95}\text{Am} \rightarrow {}^{237}_{93}\text{Np} + {}^{4}_{2}\text{He}$
 [1 mark for correct mass number and 1 mark for correct atomic number.]
12. elastic potential energy
 = 0.5 × spring constant × (extension)² or $E_e = \frac{1}{2}ke^2$
 Rearrange for k:
 $k = (2 \times E_e) \div e^2$ *[1 mark]*
 = $(2 \times 0.9) \div (0.03^2)$ *[1 mark]*
 = 2000 N/m *[1 mark]*

Test 42: Physics 1 Mixed Topics
Pages 84–85
1. B *[1 mark]*   2. B *[1 mark]*
3. A *[1 mark]*   4. B *[1 mark]*
5. C *[1 mark]*   6. B *[1 mark]*
7. A *[1 mark]*   8. A *[1 mark]*
9. diode/LED *[1 mark]*
10. alpha *[1 mark]*
 beta *[1 mark]*
11. thermal energy for a change of state = mass × specific latent heat
 = 0.25 × 111 000 *[1 mark]*
 = 27 750 J (or 28 000 J to 2 s.f.) *[1 mark]*
12. efficiency
 = useful output energy transfer ÷ total input energy transfer
 = 420 ÷ 560 *[1 mark]*
 = 0.75 (or 75%) *[1 mark]*

Physics Paper 2
Test 43: Forces
Pages 86–87
1. A *[1 mark]*   2. B *[1 mark]*
3. B *[1 mark]*   4. C *[1 mark]*
5. A *[1 mark]*   6. B *[1 mark]*
7. B *[1 mark]*   8. A *[1 mark]*
9. Terminal velocity/speed *[1 mark]*
 There is no resultant force acting on the skydiver / 0 N *[1 mark]*.
10. distance travelled = speed × time *[1 mark]*
 distance travelled
 = 3.5 × 26 *[1 mark]*
 = 91 m *[1 mark]*
11. Between C and D the object travels at a steady velocity / has an acceleration of 0 m/s² *[1 mark]*. Between D and E the object is decelerating at a constant rate *[1 mark]*.

Test 44: Forces
Pages 88–89
1. A *[1 mark]*   2. A *[1 mark]*
3. B *[1 mark]*   4. B *[1 mark]*
5. C *[1 mark]*   6. A *[1 mark]*
7. A *[1 mark]*   8. B *[1 mark]*
9. E.g. speed is a scalar quantity, velocity is a vector. / Speed is how fast an object moves, velocity is how fast it moves in a given direction *[1 mark]*.
10. Any two from: e.g. tiredness / being under the influence of drugs / being under the influence of alcohol *[1 mark for each correct answer]*
11. Work done = elastic potential energy stored
 elastic potential energy
 = 0.5 × 30 × 0.20² *[1 mark]*
 = 0.6 J *[1 mark]*

12. The speed of the car is equal to the gradient of the graph.
 Gradient = 240 ÷ 30 *[1 mark]*
 = 8 m/s *[1 mark]*
 [Or 2 marks for the correct answer via any other method]

Test 45: Forces
Pages 90–91
1. B *[1 mark]*   2. B *[1 mark]*
3. B *[1 mark]*   4. A *[1 mark]*
5. A *[1 mark]*   6. C *[1 mark]*
7. B *[1 mark]*   8. A *[1 mark]*
9. Two *[1 mark]*
 Force = spring constant × extension *[1 mark]*
10. E.g. The cyclist accelerates for the first 11 seconds / until they have travelled 28 m *[1 mark]*. The cyclist then stops and remains stationary for the next 9 seconds *[1 mark]*.
11. work done = force × distance
 Rearrange for force and substitute in the values:
 force = work done ÷ distance *[1 mark]*
 = 84 ÷ 1.2 *[1 mark]*
 = 70 N *[1 mark]*

Test 46: Waves
Pages 92–93
1. B *[1 mark]*   2. C *[1 mark]*
3. A *[1 mark]*   4. B *[1 mark]*
5. A *[1 mark]*   6. B *[1 mark]*
7. A *[1 mark]*   8. C *[1 mark]*
9. Any two from: e.g. to cook food / in infrared cameras / in electric heating *[2 marks]*.
10. Waves which oscillate at 90° to the direction of energy transfer *[1 mark]*.
11. The ripples don't carry the leaf away with them because waves don't transfer matter (only energy) *[1 mark]*.

Answers

12. E.g. double the half-wavelength measurement to find the wavelength *[1 mark]*. The frequency of the wave will be the same as the frequency set by the signal generator *[1 mark]*. The student should substitute both these values into the equation wave speed = frequency × wavelength / $v = f\lambda$ to find the speed of the wave *[1 mark]*.

Test 47: Waves
Pages 94–95
1. C *[1 mark]* 2. B *[1 mark]*
3. B *[1 mark]* 4. A *[1 mark]*
5. B *[1 mark]* 6. C *[1 mark]*
7. B *[1 mark]* 8. A *[1 mark]*
9. E.g. skin aging / increased risk of skin cancer *[1 mark]*
10. wave speed = frequency × wavelength
    = $6.0 \times 10^7 \times 1.4$
    [1 mark]
    = 8.4×10^7 m/s
    (or 84 000 000 m/s)
    [1 mark]
11. E.g.

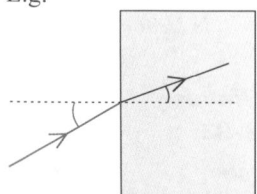

[1 mark for a ray drawn from the point of incidence, inside the block, on the opposite side of and at a smaller angle to the normal than the incident ray].

12. The first peak is at 0.01 s and the second peak is at 0.035 s, so:
    period = 0.035 – 0.01
           = 0.025 s *[1 mark]*
    frequency = 1 ÷ period
              = 1 ÷ 0.025 *[1 mark]*
              = 40 Hz *[1 mark]*
    [Or 3 marks for the correct answer via any other method.]

Test 48: Magnetism and Electromagnetism
Pages 96–97
1. A *[1 mark]* 2. B *[1 mark]*
3. A *[1 mark]* 4. C *[1 mark]*
5. B *[1 mark]* 6. B *[1 mark]*
7. A *[1 mark]* 8. B *[1 mark]*
9. A region where other magnets or magnetic materials experience a force *[1 mark]*.
10.

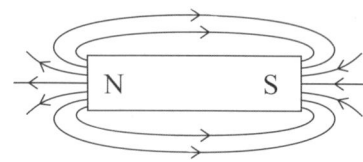

[1 mark for lines (at least 3) drawn to show the correct field shape, 1 mark for arrows drawn in correct direction on every field line.]

11. The current flowing through the wire can be increased *[1 mark]*. The wire can be shaped into a solenoid *[1 mark]*.
12. The compass will point north *[1 mark]*. This is because it aligns with the Earth's magnetic field / the magnetic field generated by the Earth's core *[1 mark]*.

Test 49: Physics 2 Mixed Topics
Pages 98–99
1. A *[1 mark]* 2. B *[1 mark]*
3. A *[1 mark]* 4. C *[1 mark]*
5. A *[1 mark]* 6. B *[1 mark]*
7. C *[1 mark]* 8. B *[1 mark]*
9. E.g. satellite communications / cooking food *[1 mark]*.
10. It would become an induced magnet / it would experience an attractive force *[1 mark]*.

11. The acceleration is equal to the gradient, so:
    acceleration
    = change in y ÷ change in x
    = 80 ÷ 10 *[1 mark]*
    = 8 m/s^2 *[1 mark]*
12. wave speed = frequency × wavelength *[1 mark]*
    8.4 cm = 0.084 m
    wave speed = 4.0×0.084 *[1 mark]*
    = 0.336 m/s
    = 0.34 m/s (to 2 s.f) *[1 mark]*

Test 50: Physics 2 Mixed Topics
Pages 100–101
1. A *[1 mark]* 2. C *[1 mark]*
3. B *[1 mark]* 4. B *[1 mark]*
5. B *[1 mark]* 6. C *[1 mark]*
7. A *[1 mark]* 8. A *[1 mark]*
9. The spring constant of the spring (in N/m) *[1 mark]*
10. Force = mass × acceleration
    = 24 × 3 *[1 mark]* = 72 N *[1 mark]*
11. The downwards force is larger than the upwards force, so the resultant force will be downwards.
    Resultant force
    = force downwards – force upwards = 750 – 600 = 150 N *[1 mark]* downwards *[1 mark]*
12. Hold an infrared detector a set distance away from one of the cube's painted faces, and record the amount of infrared radiation it detects *[1 mark]*. Repeat this measurement for the other face at the same distance from the cube and compare the two measurements *[1 mark]*.